James A. B. Dilworth

Free Banking

A Natural Right

James A. B. Dilworth

Free Banking
A Natural Right

ISBN/EAN: 9783743410312

Manufactured in Europe, USA, Canada, Australia, Japa

Cover: Foto ©Suzi / pixelio.de

Manufactured and distributed by brebook publishing software (www.brebook.com)

James A. B. Dilworth

Free Banking

FREE BANKING

A NATURAL RIGHT

BY

JAMES A. B. DILWORTH

MDCCCXCVII

CONTINENTAL PUBLISHING CO.

NEW YORK AND LONDON

PREFACE.

To the critical reader of history it is apparent that, as a nation advances in civilization and material wealth, the increase of its pauper and criminal class is at a much greater ratio than its population, and that poverty promotes crime. If this were the result of a universal law, the ratio of pauperism and crime to self-sustaining population would be equal in communities of equal population, enlightenment, and wealth.

Such, however, is not the case. Nor is it a universal law, nor, indeed, a law at all that, as communities increase in intelligence, material wealth, and in the development of the arts, poverty and crime must also increase.

In communities where natural opportunities, properly utilized, furnish in abundance the necessities and comforts of life for all, the existence of poverty and crime is not the result of a universal law; it is because of a disregard of a natural law.

It was the hope that I might do something

to imbed this truth in the minds of some of
my fellow-men that caused this monograph
to be written.

The particular lesson I wish to teach is
that the monopolization of money by nations
or by great corporations, like that of the Bank
of England, is a disregard of natural rights, a
fruitful source of injustice, a limitation of freedom to opportunity, and is most potent in
developing poverty and crime. I seek to
prove, furthermore, that money is not an
essential concomitant of commerce, but that
credit is, and that civilization can more readily
dispense with legal-tender money than with
credit money.

This is no new thought to me. More than
thirty years ago I published my first article
on this subject, and the years of thought since
then bestowed upon the theme have served
only to strengthen my belief in the correctness of the theory; namely, that the best
money to promote the welfare of communities
is money of that character that makes it acceptable to those of the community for whose
interest it is issued, and is to them of value
equal to the safest money, yet of so little intrinsic value that it will not be attracted from
the community for whose interest it was
issued.

I herein propose monetary methods founded on the Golden Rule—just to all, and unjust to none. These, put into practice, will give to each community in the United States where natural privileges abound and idle labor exists, opportunities equal to those of other communities of our country.

It will prevent innocent communities from being disastrously affected by the inequalities or the calamities of others; by it, financially weak communities could not be oppressed by financially strong communities. Because of it, great cities cannot grow and prosper at the expense of smaller cities and those of agrarian interests.

THE AUTHOR.

ERRATA.

Page 41.   Line 28.   Read "limitation," not "imitation."

Page 49.   Line 19.   Read "could fix," not "would fix."

Page 55.   Lines 2 and 3 should read : "Of its citizens for the law and in their belief in the justice of law.   So long as law," etc.

Page 62.   Line 4.   Read "arbitrary laws," not "artificial laws."

Page 82.   Line 12.   Read "restriction of," not "exercise of."

Page 98.   Line 17 is a repetition of line 13 and should be omitted, and instead read "national bank notes, bonds, stamp."

Page 139.   Line 15.   Read "apparently," not "on the other hand."

Page 182.   Line 29.   Read "being established," not "established."

Page 196.   Lines 2, 3, 4, 5 and 6, should read " activity, under the system described, the accumulation of wealth has been reserved for the people of the communities which produced it, and distributed as fairly as under any system of economy yet devised."

FREE BANKING.

CHAPTER I.

THE Presidential election of 1896 teaches in an emphatic and unmistakable manner that an abnormally large part of the American voters are thoroughly discontented with the monetary system of our country. Upward of forty-six per cent. of those voters emphasized their discontent by voting for a radical and extremely experimental departure from our established custom of monetary management, notwithstanding the fact that every dollar issued by our Government—whether of paper, silver, or gold—is worth, and is readily convertible into, 24.8 grains of gold, 900 fineness, and equal to the most reliable and staple currency of the world. Upward of 6,500,000 of our people, as intelligent, patriotic, and honest as the 7,000,000 who voted for Mr. McKinley, gave their consent to our Government to open the mints of the United States to the free and unlimited coinage of silver into silver dollars of 412½ grains of silver,

900 fineness, and to make such silver dollar legal tender for all public and all private debts.

Nearly all of these 6,500,000 of voters knew that the silver bullion in the silver dollar was worth in the markets of the world only half as much as the gold bullion contained in a gold dollar.

To assume that nearly all of those citizens who voted for Mr. Bryan did not know the relative value of the metals contained in the two coins, is a reflection on the intelligence of the American voter and on the system of education in the United States. This cannot successfully be maintained. To assume that a great proportion of those 6,500,000 of voters is dishonest, and that when giving their votes in support of free coinage of silver they sought to escape financial responsibilities, is even a greater libel on the fair name of our country, as well as on the ethical development of republican institutions.

Upon many men has been bestowed the gift of beautiful speech, and the power to array in charming language unreasonable and illogical thought. And too often also for the best interest of the whole people has this gift been used to charm the ear, to disturb thought, and to stagnate reasoning. The power of eloquence, too, has probably never been used with greater disadvantage to the people of the United States than during the last Presidential campaign.

Mr. Bryan, the nominee of the Democratic party, possesses a power to arrange and emphasize words to charm the ear that but few other orators possess; and throughout the late campaign that great gift was aided also by great personal magnetism and severe physical endurance.

Few of our public men have displayed more courage—none, perhaps, as much energy and endurance—in espousing a cause as that displayed by Mr. Bryan in his campaign for "Free Coinage of Silver." His was the energy of the enthusiast. Mere personal ambition could not have prompted such fervor of speech, such intensity of action. Like Peter the Hermit, the cause he championed he believed to be just; that its triumph would emancipate millions from a bondage more galling than that of slavery, and would destroy a power that, if not soon checked, would relegate the agricultural masses of our country to poverty more terrible, to ignorance more dense, than that of Russian serfdom.

Had his cause been triumphant, it might not have been so disastrous to his followers as was the cause of those who followed the Hermit, whose bones now form a part of the

soil from the sea-washed coast of Europe to
the banks of the Bosphorus.

It is difficult to see how any lasting benefit could come to a people from changing their
money basis from gold to silver, or from
gold to silver and gold, unless the method to
provide mediums for exchange was radically
changed. Mr. Bryan's fervent and distract-
ing eloquence is largely responsible for the
failure of those millions—discontented with
the financial condition of the country—to go
deeper into the real cause of the discontent.
To the Democratic campaign he gave the cue;
and a flood-gate of eloquence was opened,
from which outswept entrancing and distract-
ing appeals to the people. All were centered
upon the one financial remedy—free coinage
of silver. Yet the very arguments used to
win voters to the free coinage of silver, if extended to a logical conclusion, demonstrated
that free coinage was not the remedy for
existing evils.

Mr. McKinley, not so eloquent in speech,
probably, but more subtle perhaps in stage
effect, appealed to the emotional rather than
the reasoning nature of men. In this respect
he also gave the cue to the great army of orators and educators who espoused the cause of
" Sound Money " and the single standard.
The " Credit of the Nation " and " Honest

Money " were potent factors in winning voters for Mr. McKinley. Even " Old Glory " and " Patriotism " were honeyed words in the vocabulary of the Republican orators.

In the great cities, where marble and granite palaces are the homestead of many, where rich and ornate temples cover the assembled worshipers, many preachers—doubtless a number of them sincere in their belief— turned the sacred desk into a political rostrum, and, as a solemn duty of all who serve the cause of Christ, preached a new religious doctrine of " Sound Money," " The Nation's Credit," " Old Glory," " Patriotism," and " McKinley."

In communities where the homesteads consist of a few rooms made habitable by boards, lime, and sand, shutting out the breeze and cold blasts, and where pious and honest humanity worships in temples not made of stone, not ornate with gems of art, many other brethren preached that the money-changers of Jerusalem were the special aversion of the Master, and that the establishment of the single gold standard by the great nations of the world was in the interest of the money-changers, and consequently not justified by the Master. Each of these two classes of spiritual leaders preached, doubtless, that which he believed should be taught as a cardinal truth. That one or the other of these classes could not be right in their belief, it is evident. It is indeed highly probable that each was wrong. Those who believed in the righteousness of the cause, and who preached it with more or less vigor, were honest in purpose, sincerely fulfilling the solemn obligation they took upon themselves when they entered the ministry.

But those among them who introduced the discussion of the "money question" into their church work, and from the pulpit discussed "Honest Money" and "Patriotism," "The Masses and the Classes," and "Crime of '73," for the purpose of touching a chord in harmony with the views of their congregation, are the ulcers of religion, the pests of society, an affliction to mankind. The generation to follow will pity these ignorant zealots of the last campaign, and will hold in supreme contempt those who used the sacred desk for pride and gain.

The geographical division of the country into "Sound Money" and "Free Silver Coinage" communities should, of itself, be sufficient to raise a doubt in all thoughtful minds as to the correctness of the views of either of the great parties on the question of money.

Following the line along the southern boundary of Delaware to the mouth of the

Potomac River; following the course of that river to the Falls of the Potomac, and then westward to Kentucky, and along the Ohio River to the Mississippi; up that "Father of Waters" to the north boundary of Missouri, and then westward to the crest of the Sierras; along these mountains to Mexico; then following the Mexican line to the Gulf, and along the coast back to the Delaware boundary, comprises a territory of gigantic extent, populated more or less densely by a people of much intelligence, great energy, and of enormous capability. By a great majority of the voters of that immense territory the free coinage of silver, at a rate of 16 to 1 of gold, was demanded as a measure of relief from that which they doubtless believed to be the oppressive system of money, the basis of which is gold.

It displays very little intelligence, less love of country, and no sense of justice at all, to denounce the majority of the people of that great territory as ignorant, unpatriotic, or dishonest. Nor can their discontent be remedied by such criticism. For this discontent some other source must be sought than that of ignorance, disloyalty, or dishonesty. The measure of their intelligence—if gauged by the mental forces of those who met them in discussion on the hustings, in the forum, or in the press of the country—does not, on the contrary, disclose great ignorance.

Let the storm signal of the nation's danger be hoisted, and in responding to the country's call to arms, no doubt as much alacrity would be displayed by the people of those States that gave their votes to Mr. Bryan as would be shown by those States that gave their votes to Mr. McKinley. And measured by the standard of wealth, they would no doubt be equally responsive to the Government call for financial aid. The honest and dishonest proclivities of American citizens are not marked by States, nor by sections of the Republic.

Assuming that States vote as a unit in Presidential elections, 40,000,000 of the people, worth $47,390,000,000, or per capita of about $1200, gave their ratification to Mr. McKinley in support of the existing gold standard, and 22,000,000 of the people, worth $16,680,000,-000, or per capita of about $750, gave their votes to Mr. Bryan and to a free and unlimited coinage of silver into standard dollars, the bullion value of which at the time was worth only about half as much as the worth of the bullion in the gold dollar.

The figures given above are presumably correct. They were those presented recently by a great New York daily journal, to support the theory that, because the wealth of the country was so largely on the side of Mr. Mc-Kinley and the gold standard, it was the intelligence of the country that gave its support to that cause. Well may the Free Silver Coinage advocate give Dean Swift's retort to a similar proposition: " God shows his appreciation of money by the character of the man he bestows it upon."

These figures prove that the rich and affluent communities are well satisfied with the present condition; while, on the other hand, the poverty-oppressed and struggling communities are discontented. And it is a fair inference that the present conditions afford the affluent all the opportunity that they may reasonably hope to possess to hold on to their present accumulations and to increase their stores of wealth. It is equally fair also to assume that existing conditions deny to the struggling classes a fair opportunity to maintain themselves in comfort, or arouse a hope in them that they may provide themselves against want, when age incapacitates them from producing for themselves.

Those who possess large fortunes, who control the finances of the country, and largely expand or limit its credits, as their hopes or fears control them, cannot afford to treat with indifference, much less contempt, the appeals for relief from fancied or real oppression that the large vote given to Mr. Bryan seems to plead for; no matter if this oppressed condition be real or imaginary; no matter if the cause of the discontent be the result of bad management or of diseased minds. Whatever the cause, so great a number of discontented is a menace to the stability of government.

How to reconcile these discontented citizens of our country is a problem that demands the thoughtful attention of every lover of law and order. There can be no questioning of the fact that a large majority of American citizens demand that order must be maintained. This sentiment is almost unanimous. Not only do they demand preservation of order in all communities, but they insist upon it to the extent even that if the law stands in the way of its immediate enforcement, the law must violently for a time be brushed aside. It is this demand for order that prompts lynching, and, as is well known, causes men to organize such societies as Kuklux, White Caps, and associations of that character. And in the judgment of the masses of our citizens, the end nearly always justifies the means, if the end be peace and quietude.

The assembling, too, of men to hear and discuss principles of statecraft, religious, and other social problems, is encouraged by the

sentiment of our people, who are quick to resist any infringement on that right unless the
belief be prevalent that such assembling of the
people may be to advance a theory of political
science that will lead to disorder. In case of
such assembling the people are intolerant, and
in their criticism of the Government too often
are severe because it gives too much consideration to law, and, consequently, being,
in their belief, too lenient in its treatment of
such assemblings. It is indeed to be regretted that so great a number of the citizens
of the United States should prove themselves
to be " violent people." This is one of the
potent factors of American temperament that
now menace the stability of our Government.

It will be impossible to maintain the present
standard of education, much less advance it,
if freedom of thought is to be crushed. Nor
does it alone require Bastiles and Siberian
mines to repress it. Social ostracism is even
more potent to do so than prison walls or
Siberian ice-wastes.

The growing tendency of the well-to-do
citizens of the United States, and of their army
of satellites, to class all who differ with them
on the great social problems as anarchists and
socialists is much to be lamented. Doubtless
only a small proportion of those who so
flippantly use those terms to describe their

neighbors and fellow-citizens have the remotest idea of what anarchism or socialism really means. When using such terms they wish to be offensive only, and there is about the same amount of intelligence displayed when using them, or less, even, than by those persons who describe the great Adversary as a man with horse's hoofs and bull's horns, who feasts on live coals, and washes them down with libations of liquid sulphur in a fiery state.

Men, by their environment left free to think and to express their thoughts to their fellowmen, will not unite in concerted action on any one line of thought, nor worship at any one shrine, nor be bound by any one creed; yet if left free to think and speak, the same men will unite on ethical lines along highways of justice and truth. There are but few of our countrymen who, convinced that those principles of government that they have advocated are not calculated to increase the national welfare, but, on the contrary, to detract from it, but what will quickly abandon the advocacy of those principles. The number of citizens who seek, either by direct or subtle means, to impair the welfare of our common country is so infinitesimal as to be an incalculable factor in the nation's affairs.

On the contrary, to anyone who will give a thought to this proposition, the wholesale charges of dishonesty and disloyalty against those millions of our people who opposed the election of Mr. McKinley, must appear not only absurd, but almost criminal. How many of those who so delighted to speak of Mr. Bryan as an insincere seeker after fame and fortune, who called Governor Altgeld an anarchist, Senators Morgan and Jones repudiationists, and Senators Teller and Stewart plunderers, have ever realized the extent of the degeneration of the agriculturist's hope since 1860?

A full generation has passed away since then, but thousands now live in health and vigor whose memory carries them back to years even before 1860. They well remember the joyous expectancy that filled the souls of the young couple who began life upon a mortgaged farm, with only their good health and energy, a few horses, cows, fowls, pigs, and old farming utensils as capital. Experience of others had taught them that only a lack of health and an unnatural shortening of the life of the farmer, and the absence of sobriety and energy on his part, would prevent them from attaining the full ownership of that farm; that, in fact, free from all detracting incumbrances, with many improvements that would add to its fertility and to their comforts, they would greatly increase its market value should they desire to sell it. That farm was to them what the savings banks are to the wage-earner. The labor they expended on its improvements only increased their store to provide for their comforts when years should incapacitate them from further productiveness. It was indeed this hope, born of the experiences of their fathers, that in forty years turned the wild prairies of Ohio, Illinois, and Indiana into fertile fields rich with grain and grass. It built up the great West without the aid of capitalists. In one generation it established on the plains, over which wild beasts and wilder men had roamed, a territory vast and densely populated with happy, prosperous, and hopeful agriculturists.

To those who dwell in cities! Does the thought ever occur that, if measured by the standard of gold dollars, scarcely a farm in the thirteen original States, or in those new States created solely by the energy, nerve, and logical hope in the hearts of young farmers, could have been sold for as much—the improvement being equal—on any succeeding New Year as on a preceding year since the year 1860 unless some special local value had been given to it by a new industry available to only the few?

Do those worthy citizens who dwell in towns and cities and deal in commodities of the farm, who have grown richer year by year during the past thirty-five years, and who have seen that real estate upon which they transacted their business and upon which they live, increase year by year in selling value, realize what would be the probable condition of their minds had they, after a struggle of a lifetime, reached old age, or an age of crippled energy, only to find themselves unprovided for, the real estate on which they did business practically unsalable, their homestead valueless?

To thoroughly understand the trend of mind of the voters of purely agricultural communities, one must put oneself into the same conditions that the farmer now finds himself in.

A good ship sails over summer seas laden with a precious freight of human lives and their treasures; the gentle swelling of the waves and the balmy breezes blowing over deck make existence upon her most delightful. Over her quarter the water is churned into cream by the rapid turning of her propeller; and all on board are happy and contented. In comfort and safety they are speeding toward that haven that they hope soon to find. Not a cloud is to be seen in the sky; not a breath of air save that which the ship's onward motion creates. On the far-distant horizon a small dark spot presents itself to the few whose eyes are trained to seek just such premonition of coming storms.

The ship and time speed on, and all eyes on shipboard soon see the little dark spot. Some believe it to be the vanguard cloud of an impending storm; others that it is an island; others that it is a great ship. All are honest in their separate convictions. Each has seen, by natural processes of brain and optic nerves, what each has described. It is certain that all convictions cannot be right. In that case one alone could be correct—perhaps none.

In a little time, however, no one would be left in doubt. The black clouds will present themselves so distinctly to their vision that all soon will know that a storm threatens them with destruction. The government of a ship at sea is that of an autocrat, and the maneuvering of the ship is the work of its commander. Upon his ability as a seaman, upon his fidelity, depend, in any given impending danger, the safety of his government, the lives and comfort of its people, the security of the wealth within the ship's boundaries.

Suppose the ship be not under autocratic control; suppose it be that of a democratic community in which all on board are equally interested in the welfare of its freight of human lives and communal wealth; should those who saw in that little speck on the horizon an island or a ship, be forever disfranchised from having a voice in the control of the affairs of that ship? Should they be condemned to any degradation or distress for their failure to see aright? Surely he who would assert the affirmative of such a proposition cannot be a good citizen of a republican institution, no matter if perfectly honest himself in such belief. Does any man see an unworthy and dishonest cause for doubting the integrity and earnestness of those who failed to see that the little speck was a cloud? If he does, then his own reasoning is faulty, and he is unfitted to be a critic of other men's motives.

Upon that ship, where all are equal in authority, suppose the majority should determine that the best seamanship demanded that the helm be ported, would it be good policy, would it be just, would it be kindly, would it be even good, hard, common horsesense for that majority to declare and reiterate that those who wanted to starboard the helm were anarchists, knaves, repudiationists, destructionists, numskulls, and ignorant hayseeds? Would it mend matters? Would it enable the ship to weather with more ease and security the next storm that might arise?

And who can tell how soon that storm will come; with what a fury it will rage? Forty thousand men may stand viewing an ap-

proaching storm.   There may be a division of
opinion as to whether the storm will burst
upon them; but no one will dispute the existence of the clouds, or that their appearance
portends a storm.   On the question of how
best to protect themselves from the fury of the
storm there will be many opinions; but each
opinion may be the honest expression of a desire that all shall escape from a calamity that
possibly threatens them all.

A fire started on the prairies by some care-
less hunter, discloses itself to a little band of
travelers; all at once recognize its presence
and its danger.   The swift-blowing breezes
sweep it rapidly toward them.   Safety, in their
opinion, can be assured only by starting another fire and by keeping to the windward of
the newly-started conflagration till sufficient
space has been burned over in front of them.
On this they may stand in safety from the
oncoming fire.   By their act of starting a fire
they have endangered the lives and property
of those beyond.

But who is it can truthfully say that, had
his environment been that of those travelers,
he would not have done likewise?   The most
impressive law of nature is that of self-preser-
vation; and those endangered prairie-travel-
ers can be held no more accountable for the
destruction to life and property that the fire

they had kindled might cause, than can those who in the last Presidential election gave their votes to Mr. McKinley, believing that the election of his opponent meant the destruction of their business and of their hope in life; or, on the other hand, than those who gave their votes to Mr. Bryan, believing that the election of his opponent meant the continuance of monetary methods that were responsible, they believed, for the grinding poverty they felt themselves, their friends, and fellow-countrymen to be afflicted with.

CHAPTER II.

THE cause of the rapid massing of great bodies of humanity into phenomenally large cities during the last century, is a problem that has been a fruitful source of prolific study and discussion by political economists. Doubtless the great increase of facilities for rapid and economic transportation, thereby making the victualing of the people of such cities as London, New York, Paris, Berlin, and other great centers, not only a possible but an easy task, has had much to do with the development of those cities. But rapid and economical transportation was by no means the cause of such growth. It only made such growth possible.

The harnessing of the subtle forces of nature,—as steam and electricity,—and the making of them obedient to the will of man, have made it possible for the crude materials for the manufacturing arts to be brought cheaply to the great cities, and there formed into the various articles that the needs of humanity demand, and are again distributed as naturally required, thus giving employment to the dwellers in the cities. But the mere fact of it being possible to give employment to the dwellers in cities does not constitute a cause for people huddling into them, as they have been doing during the last century.

Man is essentially a social animal, and, when mentally normal, seeks the companionship of his fellow-men. He is a progressive animal, too, and seeks for enlightenment wherever his judgment leads him to believe he can find it.

Here again we have an important factor in the building of villages, towns, and cities; although not a sufficient one. But, after all, it is not because of the ease by which food may be got to them, nor because natural forces have been harnessed by man, and made subservient to his will, nor for social advantages, that the young, intelligent, and active men go from the farms and the villages to the great cities; it is rather because they believe that rewards for effort put forth by them are greater in the cities than in the country. It is not the allurement of the tinsel and gold of the cities, nor is it so much the more generous food supply, the more pleasant companionship, that attracts them; it is more generally the glowing pictures of ease and comfort of the cities, portrayed to them by those of their acquaintances who, at some time more or less recent, had, like themselves, labored in the country, but, unlike them, to mend their fortune had gone away to the city. There they had met with fair success, and had come back well clothed and apparently well kept, to enjoy a short holiday of rest.

If those thousands of young men who are now so anxious to change their country homes for homes in the city could but feel with the same confidence that their efforts to secure a fortune in their country homes would be equally rewarded as that hope born of the evidence of prosperity of their kind who have gone to the cities bids them believe will be their reward in the cities, not one in a hundred would ever think of leaving the friends and associates of childhood and youth for the dazzling brilliancy of the cities. Those who change their dwelling places from the country to the city are almost invariably induced to that act because they believe that the problem of how to maintain life with the greatest ease is more readily and more satisfactorily solved in the cities than in the country.

As water fallen from the skies to the highlands finds its way to the sea along lines that offer the least resistance, so does man seek for his subsistence along those lines that afford him the greatest ease. From the dawn of civilization all records seem to support the affirmation that tilling the soil has ever been the most laborious, the least exciting, and least attractive occupation of man. Under ordinarily favorable conditions it has been healthful, and man has developed brawn and brainpowers under its influence. The fields and farms have throughout the ages furnished to mankind the spirit of progression from which very largely has come that development that has transformed man from a nomad to that high enlightenment he has attained, and it is now a debatable question whether man, exclusively under the influence and the culture of the civilization that directs the ethics of great cities, would not become a degenerate. The ages may be called as convincing witnesses to prove that the fields and farms have no such fatal influence. The progressive man among the agriculturists who selects some field for his talents other than that of cultivating the soil, may progress more rapidly by going to the cities to pursue studies, because there he will find a greater opportunity for investigation. He will find also allurements to lead him from his work into avenues of ease and pleasure, which, if he does not resist, will vitiate the progressive spirit within him.

It is not necessary, however, to draw a comparison between the merits of humanity on farms and humanity in cities, much less to glorify one, or to disparage the other. To awaken the public to the fact that the agriculturists of the world have always, under fair conditions, been decidedly progressive, is, on the other hand, desirable.

Success is an unsatisfactory criterion of excellence, but to be uniformly successful is certainly strong evidence of superiority, and the successes of the children of the farm in all the various phases of human struggles for supremacy have been quite marked. It is absurd to deny, on the score of lack of intellect, to the tillers of the soil the right to claim equal privileges in affairs of state.

There is a vast difference in the meaning of the terms intelligence and intellect, although the one is frequently used as the synonym of the other. A dull mind may, by careful culture, be developed to a degree of knowledge that may enable it to reason with force and even vigor. But such mind must be continually forcing the sense of memory to an inordinate energy. That in a measure affects the power of that mind. The possessors of such minds may truly be classed as intelligent. But intellect is a gift, something born with the body, and which, unaided, will cause the soul or will of such a body to seek for information or intelligence. An intelligent mind does not stand upon the same plane with an intellectual mind. Intelligence is acquired. Intellect is a gift. The intelligent mind in pursuit of knowledge may, under more favorable conditions, surpass the intellectual mind; but, all things being equal, it will always be behind it in the struggle for mental supremacy or progress.

Hygienics is as essential to mental development as are training schools. A diseased body may contain a highly developed mind, but the seed of that body most generally develops a degenerate. Hothouse plants are frequently more brilliant than those produced in the open air, but they are never so hardy, and the seed of the hothouse plant almost universally produces a degenerate of its species. Does this not teach a wholesome lesson? May it not be that much of the brilliancy in the minds of those reared in the cities is the result of the hothouse-forcing system of education prevalent in the cities, and, like other hothouse plants, may the seed be not more certainly depended upon to produce a degenerate than otherwise?

It is undeniable that a very large proportion of those men who have stamped their names indelibly on the pages of recorded history have been those whose earlier opportunities for education have been limited by rural environ-

ments, and who, in spite of these limited means
for acquiring knowledge, have become great
in all the various professions and avocations of
life.   There is no good reason now for sup-
porting the theory that there has in recent
years been any degeneration of the mental
capabilities of rural populations.

Nor can the theory that there has been any
marked mental progression among the inhabitants of the great city be successfully
maintained.

Unless indeed it can be successfully maintained that the rural population of the United
States are degenerates, and that the population of towns and cities are progressive, it is
not only unwise, it is absolutely senseless, to
maintain that the great mass of American voters were not controlled in their voting by
sense of reason when, by their votes, they gave
their consent to the free coinage of silver by
the mints of the United States.

It is quite possible that a great majority of
those who consented to the free coinage of
silver by our Government believed that free
coinage alone was not the remedy, but that
the monetary methods of the present time
were oppressive to the struggling industrial
classes, and that free coinage of silver was a
step in the direction of a reform that they believed necessary for the commonweal.

Had they no cause to believe that a reform in the monetary system of our country is a necessity? That necessity has been recognized by every Congress assembled in Washington since the War of the Rebellion, and it must indeed be a dull mind that did not perceive in the currency panic of 1893, and in the rapid depletion of the Treasury of its gold in 1895-96, a most serious defect in our monetary system.

Examine for a moment the plain facts of the currency panic of 1893. In that year there was somewhere hidden, or in use, in the United States $1,111,720,898 of paper money, the redemption of which was guaranteed by the United States. In addition to this, there was, according to the reports of the Treasury Department, in use or in reserve throughout this country, in gold and silver coins and bullion,—all serving the purpose of money,—$1,213,413,584, or a total money supply of 2,325,134,482. Statistics of the money supply were prepared by the Treasury Department showing that there was a per capita circulation of nearly $15 in paper money alone in the United States. No thoughtful man will doubt that ample money had been provided for all business demands of the country. But the monetary methods of the country were so defective, that but a small part of this vast issue of currency could be made available by the people. For some undefinable reason, or insane impulse, the whole nation, as one man, seemed suddenly to become impressed with the conviction that there would in the very near future be a great scarcity of currency bills.

This impulse could not have been the result of a distrust of the silver certificates, or because of silver legislation, because the silver certificates were with the greenbacks, national bank and coin notes, carefully concealed in the safety-deposit vaults, and between the leaves of the family Bible, and other similar secure hiding places. The silver dollar bill commanded a premium in gold on the counters of the money dealers. The gold and silver, coin and bullion, in the vaults of the Government could not be moved but to meet current expenses of the Government; hence it was practically not money in circulation. Probably sixty per cent. of the paper money of the country was hidden from circulation.

It is quite probable that at the time of the greatest contraction of currency in 1893, there was not in circulation in the entire country more than $400,000,000 of money available for business purposes. What remained of the money of the country was securely withheld from the public. Within six weeks from that time confidence had been restored, the insane had become rational, the intoxicated returned to sobriety, and the entire mass of hidden bills were again put into circulation. Within six months the credit of the country had oscillated from vigorous health to the verge of dissolution, and was again restored to its full and healthy vigor. Within that time the currency had been contracted nearly or quite sixty per cent., then suddenly expanded to its extreme bounds.

Can any country prosper, can its finances ever be healthy, when such conditions may threaten it at any time? Tariff legislation, presumably an innocent business of Congress to provide revenues for government, has for many years menaced the stability of business affairs in the United States, and Congress may at any time, in the course of natural and necessary legislation, cause a contraction of the currency, either of its paper or its coins, by simply starting an alarm that will send the bills or the coins, as the case may be, into the safe deposit vaults, or old stocking, or between the leaves of the family Bible.

The financial scare of 1895-96 was the result of a fear by those rich enough to be lenders of money that the purchasing power of the dollar, in the event of our Government

opening its mints to the free coinage of silver,
would be decreased, and that they would be
compelled to receive, in payment for their
loans, less value than they gave.

It is difficult to find in their reasoning any
error on this question. Thousands of those
who could afford to buy gold and hide it,
did so: some from a sense of security, others
from purely speculative motives. Banks, to
a very great extent, substituted in their vaults
gold for bills for the reserved funds, and private citizens, to a very great extent, locked it
in safe-deposit vaults. "Here a little and
there a little" of the gold coins of the country was hidden away, until practically the entire coined gold supply of the country was
effectively withdrawn from public use. Twice
the gold reserve of the country was depleted
to an extent that impaired the credit of the
country. The third time, two months before
the last Presidential election, the Treasury
came nearer being depleted of its gold than
ever before; so much so that it became apparent to the dealers in money, and to the
bankers of the country, that any attempt by the
Government, by bond-selling, to again replen-
ish the Treasury with gold, would result
either in turning the Government over to
those who favored free coinage of silver, or so
disastrously affect our credit that the whole

system of American securities would be sadly impaired.

It was therefore necessary for the banks to demonstrate to the public that they were doing business on a sound basis, and were abundantly able to come to the aid of the Government. This they at once did—which they could easily have done eighteen months before. By simply exchanging gold for Government paper money, silver certificates included, they furnished the Government with the necessary gold to maintain its reserve. The rapid rise in the value of wheat, caused by the great demand for American wheat in foreign countries, has since made it easy for the Government to maintain its gold reserve.

But wheat, the very cause of relief to the Treasury, and, at a critical moment, so great a help to the credit of the country, is, notwithstanding, a menace to the permanency of that credit. When India, Russia, and the Argentine Republic again produce great crops of that cereal, those who deal in money for a profit, will see a possibility of our paper money —the basis of which is silver dollars—being worth less than a gold dollar; they will then begin insidiously to deplete the Treasury of its gold, unless this or the next Congress conclude that governments should not do banking business, and provide, thereby, for its discontinuance by the United States.

But upon what can we base a hope that Congress will commit so wise an act of legislation? Certainly not by the records of that body for the last forty years; not by the platform of principles promulgated by any of the parties and factions of the last year.

The nearest approach to a decided declaration against the Government engaging in a banking business was made by the National Democracy at Indianapolis. But so long as any government uses all its powers of government to dictate what kind of paper money shall be used as money, and also guarantees the redemption of such money in the most valuable coined money of the country, so that such money shall at all times and at any point within the limits of that government be equal in value to the standard, and by prohibition or taxation prohibits the use of any other kind of paper money, that government remains in the banking business, and to the disadvantage, too, of the industries of that country.

The powers of the Federal Congress are defined by the Constitution. The Constitution provides that Congress shall have power " to coin money, regulate the value thereof and of foreign coins, and fix the standard of weights and measures."

It would be impossible to frame a paragraph in the English language that would more concisely express its meaning than that relating to the powers of Congress in relation to money. The concluding sentence, relating to weights and measures, declares beyond the possibility of a doubt that the framers of the Constitution intended that Congress should have no power over the money of the country other than to coin the precious metals and define what each coin should consist of, and what its relative value to the standard should be. To Congress was given the power to establish a standard of money, of weight, and of measures.

That the power of Congress was limited to such specific work in regard to money was not seriously disputed until 1865. The Secretary of the Treasury, Mr. Chase,—who was largely instrumental in inducing Congress to issue greenbacks,— did not believe, never pretended to believe, that Congress had the power to stamp a piece of paper and make it a legal tender. This fact was shown later in his opinion when, as Chief Justice of the United States, he decided the legal-tender legislation to be unconstitutional.

If Congress, under the imitations of Article First, Section 8, and Paragraph 5, of the Federal Constitution, is given the power to fix a value at which public and private creditors must accept any piece of paper or coin in payment of money owed to them, they have the right also to increase or diminish the weights and measures. They can declare that eight ounces shall constitute a pound, and that six inches shall measure a foot. All unfulfilled contracts calling for those things sold by weight and measures would be settled, except by concession, by the new scales of weights and measures, and every man who had contracted to buy would thereby be robbed.

Is there a sane man in America who will assert as his belief, that the Supreme Court of the United States, as constituted since its organization, would ever have asserted the constitutionality of laws that state untruths? It is manifest that a law that declared six inches to be a foot, or eight ounces to be a pound, would be an untruth.

Would it not be most unjust if a law that provided that those who had made contracts, prior to the passing of the law, for 1000 feet of piping for delivery at some future time,— which proved to be subsequent to the passage and enforcement of the new law,—should, nevertheless, make it mandatory to accept in satisfaction of such contracts the delivery of 500 feet of piping because the new law had declared 6000 inches and not 12,000 inches to be the equivalent of 1000 feet? It would be robbery to compel those who had contracted for the delivery of a ton of coal, to accept in satisfaction of such a contract the delivery of 1000 pounds of coal because the new law had declared 16,000 and not 32,000 ounces to be the equivalent of a ton.

To reduce the value of the metal in the coins and, by legal-tender enactments, to force them on the creditors of the country would, at any time in the history of our country, have been held by our Supreme Court to be unconstitutional.

Is there anyone who seriously doubts this proposition?

But the Supreme Court, asserting a legislative power never given to it by the Constitution, overturned all precedents, and declared that Congress possesses the power to have stamped on a piece of paper of no intrinsic value the words " one dollar," and make its debt-paying power equal to that of the gold dollar of the United States. Under that decision Congress may have printed enough paper dollars to pay off its indebtedness. By the time the Government have issued two or three thousand millions of such dollars, and been making a few payments in this kind of money to the Supreme Court Judges, that

honorable body will perhaps more earnestly
study the Constitution of our country and thus
arrive at the agreement that coining money
does not mean printing on paper.

There are certain scandals, of course, the
less said of them the better will morals be
promoted. That legal-tender decision may
be one of them. But may it not be well for
those who have received the benefits.of that
decision, and those who sustain it as a patriotic measure growing out of the necessities of
our country, not to throw stones too violently
at that Chicago fabric known as the Democratic platform of 1896? One of its planks
emphatically indorses the issuing of paper
money as not only a delegated power of Congress, but declares it also to be the duty of
the Government to do so to the exclusion of
all other paper money. By direct assertion
the Chicago platform protests against the use
of national-bank paper issue, and by its silence
on the subject it in a measure opposes State
and private-bank paper money.

CHAPTER III.

DURING the heat of the canvass of the late Presidential elections the candidate of the Republican party, with masterly stage effect, apparently, gave utterance to the declaration that, we must have "a dollar as sound as the Government, and as untarnished as its honor."

There may be a great uncertainty as to the meaning of that utterance of Mr. McKinley if he did not intend it for dramatic effect, but if he really meant what he said, then his dollar of the United States, to be at all times "as sound as the Government and as untarnished as its honor," would be somewhat elastic, not in the quantity but in the quality.

When the Government issued its first greenback currency, compelling the creditors of the country to receive it in payment of amounts due both from Government and private individuals, and refused to receive it for taxes due to the nation, the Government, it is true, issued money "as sound as the Government and as untarnished as its honor." And this, according to history, appears to have been worth, judged by the standard of gold, somewhere between one and sixty per cent. below par. The different rates of discount varied as the Government's prospects of life or death presented itself to that honored body of public benefactors and citizens of the world—the money-lenders.

Again, in 1893, this same band of philanthropists had become so firmly impressed with the stability of the Government that they were induced to consider the various bills of the United States currency—especially of the smaller denominations—as commodities too precious to be used for such base purposes as paying debts, excepting debts of honor and for labor; and so these same philanthropists bought the various currency bills and stowed them away, thus creating a corner in currency, just as " vulgar speculators " in the necessities of life buy corn and wheat to store, to create a corner in breadstuff. But, on that occasion, was it the paper dollar or the gold dollar that was " sound and untarnished "? Who among the voters of the country shall say which of the two dollars now issued in metal—the gold or the silver dollar—is, or is not, " a dollar as sound as the Government and as untarnished as its honor." Shall it be those millions who voted for Mr. Bryan, and, presumably, for free coinage of silver and for the silver dollar as a standard? Or shall it be those other millions who voted for and elected Mr. McKinley, and, presumably, demanded that the gold dollar should be the standard of value in the United States? Who shall or shall not determine whether the honor of the country was or was not tarnished when a Congress, elected by the people at an election when the money question was hardly considered, voted to demonetize silver—a measure by which the creditor class would have all to gain and nothing to lose; while, on the contrary, the debtor class had all to lose and nothing to gain by such demonetization? Shall it be the cohorts of Mr. Bryan, or of Mr. McKinley?

Silver and gold are commodities and not money when in the form of bullion. They are commodities of which for ages the principal use has been for money, or as a basis for money. For ages the value of the gold and silver coins has been determined by the bullion value of the gold or silver the coins contained. As commodities each was used for the same common purpose—to furnish a convenient method for the exchange of commodities. Had there been no gold in the world, the world's demand for silver for the purposes of money would have been much greater; consequently, the purchasing power of a

pound of silver would have been greater.
Had there been no silver in the world, the purchasing power of a pound of gold would have
been greater.

In many parts of the United States it is not
an uncommon thing to find a mule and a
horse hitched together drawing a load, which,
by their united efforts, they move readily. If
the public demanded that only horses should
be used to pull such loads, it is evident that
in those communities where like conditions
exist an increased demand for horses would be
created, and the demand for mules would be
decreased. And so, to extend the figure, if
the world should unite in proscribing the
mule and demanding the horse, the value of
horses would vastly increase, and the mule
would manifestly have only such value as the
curio-seeker and the arts might give it.
Were, indeed, the production of horses limited
in line with the limitation of gold productions,
the value of that animal would be vastly increased. Why does not the law of supply
and demand, which governs one division of
the world's commodities, apply to all other
sets of similar commodities?

It does apply; and to gold and silver, it also
applies; and so by the demonetization of silver by the great commercial nations, the
value of gold was enhanced; its purchasing

powers were increased, while those of silver were decreased.

It is possible that, had the commercial nations made no effort to demonetize silver, that metal, in comparison with gold, might have fallen during the last twenty years, but not to the great extent it has declined. It is, therefore, not unreasonable to believe that, if all the great commercial nations of the world were to open their mints to the free coinage of both silver and gold, the demand of the debt-payers for the cheaper metal,—silver,— and consequently a depressed market for gold for purpose of coinage, would very shortly drive the gold-bullion holders to offer their bullion—gold—for coinage. For, by thus giving to the debtor class the option of these two metals with which to pay their debts, those nations would fix the ratio of one ounce of gold to ten ounces of silver.

But so long as a half dozen of the greater commercial nations demonetize silver, it can- not, in all probability, be rehabilitated by the United States as money at a ratio with gold satisfactory to the commercial world. For so long as those great trading nations accept silver at only its bullion value, its value, meas- ured by that of gold, will continue to fluctuate to an extent too great to be accepted by the traders of the gold-standard nations as the measure by which the commodities that they sell to the silver-standard nations shall be paid; while, on the other hand, the fluctuation of the value of gold, measured by that of silver, will also vary to such an extent that traders in the silver-standard nations will be greatly inconvenienced in their business operations. Importers of silver-standard nations would be in no better condition than would be the importers of gold-standard nations. International trade, consequently, would be very greatly interfered with. And any interference with international trade is to the disadvantage of the people affected by it; though it be a people that has reached but the condition of semi-civilization; while it is to the greater disadvantage of those who accept the least used and least convenient and least forcible money standard.

There can be no great exporting nation that is not also a great importing nation. That wise member of the present Congress who, in his campaign literature, announced that he was in favor of " the world's market for American workmen, and not for the pauper labor of Europe," wrote himself down an unthinking man when he made that his battle cry. Nevertheless, owing to the blind bigotry, the unreasonable passion, and the asinine proclivities of his constituency, and also the fact that his competitors were of the same kind with but slight variations, he was, unfortunately for his country, elected.

That the people of the United States could live and be progressive and prosperous if surrounded by an impassable barrier may be conceded to be a fact, were climatic influences to remain the same. That they would not enjoy the same comforts, nor progress as rapidly in the arts and in science, is also a truth that a few thoughtful moments will fully corroborate.

Nearly every part of the world contributes to the pleasures of the breakfast of even the poorer of the workingmen of the United States. Tea, coffee, the condiments, and much of the sugar, without which that breakfast would be very unsatisfactory, come to us from foreign lands. These contributions are in exchange for those products of which we have an excess; while the contributions of foreign lands to the pleasure and comforts of the well-paid and the rich among our citizens are much greater. The United States might be rich if it were a world to itself, but it would become much richer by having that world enlarged; providing that, in the enlargement, new conditions of climate, new soil and culture were added.

No civilization has ever been, nor ever will

be, satisfied with the productions of the territory within which that civilization exists.   No
environments have ever been placed about
man that did not create within him the desire
to surmount or overcome them.   The greater
man's enlightenment, the more intense is his
desire to overcome enforced environment.
To restrict man by legislation from the exercise of his natural right is at once to make
of him a secret or open rebel against the government so restricting him.   In a popular government like that of the United States, or of
the States of the Republic, it is impossible to
enforce a law that is contrary to public opinion.   This is a perfectly apparent proposition,
which, happily, few minds fail to accept as
truth.   Yet many of our philanthropists and
statesmen have evidently failed to grasp it
when applied to certain features or conditions.
The result is, the statute books of the States of
the United States and of the general Government are crowded with unpopular laws that
have become dead letters, no attempt ever
being made to enforce them.   There they remain, monuments to the impotency of minori-
ties and to the imbecility of legislators. Moreover, they are harmful, a menace to morals,
and alas! too frequently, a lever in the hands
of the unscrupulous wise to oppress the timid
innocent.

Around that spot upon this globe that civilization has determined to be the North Pole, the eternal ages have placed a barrier of snow and ice, guarded by a cruelly frigid atmosphere. So far that barrier has resisted all attempts of man to surmount the spot. Of all the men who have endured the awful suffering in their effort to reach the North Pole, no man has been actuated to the frightful task by any hope that beyond those barriers there was a land where conditions for living would be an improvement over lands easily accessible to him and without privations of any kind. All may have been encouraged by the hope that, if successful, they would receive the plaudits of their fellow-men; that their names would be sent down the ages on the recorded pages of time, along with other great discoverers; but the controlling motive of that spirit, which will yet surmount those barriers, is the same motive that has actuated man in all his struggles to reach a position on the heights of fame loftier than that hitherto achieved by his fellow-man. And the greater the environments, the greater the determination to surmount them. Man feels it to be his natural right to possess himself of anything that his judgment tells him it would be to his benefit to have. Education and association have taught him that his right to possess that which his heart desires, must be limited to the possession of those things that do not rob his fellow-man of a possession. Hence, man has a natural right to anything attainable by him not the possession of some other man.

It is readily assumable, therefore, that the North Pole belongs to no man. Neither does trade belong to any one man. The right to trade justly with his fellow-men, in a manner commonly agreed upon, to buy in the cheapest and to sell in the dearest markets is man's natural right, and any restriction by government of those natural rights will be resisted by him. He will do it openly if he believe it to be to his interest to do so; secretly, if that method be to his advantage. His condition in life may be pleasant, his respect for law deep-seated, and his temptation to infract the law be slight. In the last case he may even obey a law the enforcement of which would have no bearing upon his condition in life. But as soon as he feels that the enforcement of such a law is a disadvantage to him and restricts him in the exercise of his natural rights, he becomes, to a greater or less extent, discontented, and his respect for law will be measurably decreased; and too frequently it becomes so decreased that his respect for law will be changed to a contempt for law.

The only hope, then, for the permanency of

constitutional government rests on the respect of its citizens for the law. And in their belief in the justice of the law, so long as a law remains in the statutes of the country, the abridgment of any natural right of man by the laws of such government becomes a menace to the permanency of that government.

Perhaps no set of legislators, either of the States or of the Nation, could serve their countrymen in any way better than by devoting the entire time of a term of such an office in efforts to repeal laws. The country can well afford to get on for a few years without new legislation, much as new legislation is needed, if it can thereby get rid of those pernicious laws that restrict its citizens from the exercise of natural rights.

Man's most important and most restricted natural right is to trade with his fellow-man and fellow-men in any way, and with the use of any convenience, that those immediately interested may commonly agree upon, so long as the methods and the conveniences do not deprive any persons of their natural rights.

This is the particular natural right of man that the government of civilization has most restricted. And from that persistent and pernicious interference with the conveniences of exchange by nearly all the governments of the world during the past two hundred years, and by the Latin nations for upward of two thousand years, has come the greater part of that degrading poverty that has ever increased in degradation and extent as arts, science, and the industries have been developed.

By the study of the experience of commercial nations the political economist formulates economic laws. Gresham's law was formulated by that financier and economist, from whom it takes its name, after years of patient study of the effect of the debased money of England upon the money not debased.

But to establish a proposition in economics into a law of economics by study of conditions is not possible, unless those conditions can be sustained as a logical sequence. If the experience of most of the progressive nations were to be accepted as establishing economical laws, a law might readily be formulated that the experiences of nations would sustain, to the effect: "That in proportion as nations increase in wealth and refinement, poverty and crime increase, and virtue and honesty decrease." It is not necessary to waste time in attempting to prove that such a preposterous proposition is not a law of nature. It is so absurd that the dullest of human minds will by intuition know it to be illogical, and consequently not a law of anything, but rather a result of the application by the controlling nations of the world of injustice and disregard of natural laws to the methods of government. And in no other way is this injustice and disregard of natural laws more flagrantly enforced than in the governmental control of the monetary affairs of the people.

Under the freest banking system ever enjoyed by the people of the United States, the number of paupers and criminals in the country was scarcely a disturbing factor, being less than two hundred and fifty to each one hundred thousand of its population. Under the supposed improved banking laws that now control our monetary system, the number of paupers and criminals to each one hundred thousand of our population has increased to upward of three thousand, and, in addition to this charge upon the public, upward of a million of our people are honorary pensioners of Government.

Under the free banking system the tramp was unknown.

Under the improvements that the ablest and most disinterested class of our fellow-citizens, the experts in banking laws, have been able to devise, the army of tramps have so increased that there is scarcely a highway in the United

States that is not in use by them. And these tramps are not enumerated either as paupers or criminals, unless they have been either inmates of jails or of almshouses. Their presence, moreover, is a menace both to person and property, and the unprotected females on almost any of the highways of the land are more fearful of them than of savage beasts. The tramp is not a self-invented, self-developed, self-made brute; he is an evolution, and society is responsible for his brutalization, and the monetary laws of civilization have had the greater part in that evolution. The criminals, too, are largely the products of bad legislation.

Who are the paupers? They are mostly of that class who are too honest to steal, and not intellectually or physically strong enough to win their own support in the struggle for existence. They yield to what they believe to be the inevitable; surrender their liberty, and voluntarily seek the imprisonment of the almshouse that they may be sheltered.

Against what? The injustice of existing laws.

Several of the almshouses of our country prove the truth of this proposition in being made self-sustaining by the united labor of their inmates. Sussex County, Delaware, was at one time in its history swept by the waters of the ocean. By ages of unceasing energy of the sea a sand bar was formed, that in time emerged from the ocean and became covered with vegetation. Its soil is thin and offers no seductive encouragement to the agriculturist. Yet by cultivation, aided by fair intelligence, and without exhausting labor, man in that county may make for himself a delightful existence.

In one of the poorest sections of that county is located the "poor farm," which contains about two hundred acres of land, upon which is situated the almshouse of the county. The population of the county is about forty thousand souls. Land is cheap and more accessible to its people than land in sections of the country where Nature makes it much easier for the agriculturist to produce his requirements. It offers but little inducement to the land speculator. This probably explains the fact that but forty-one of its inhabitants surrendered their personal liberty and voluntarily were inmates of the almshouse last year.

Certainly those forty-one paupers in the Sussex County almshouse cannot be possessed of greater energy and intellect than the average denizens of the poorhouses of our country. It is fair to assume that their energy and intelligence are below the average; nevertheless, by the wise management of that almshouse, those paupers were given an opportunity to labor and produce, by cultivating the land of the poor farm. The result is, they ceased to be paupers and became worthy, self-sustaining people.

The Sussex County Almshouse in 1895 was not only self-sustaining, but returned a profit to the county—the result of the labors of its inmates. Upon that farm were grown those commodities that could be produced upon it, not only more than enough for the wants of the inmates, but the sale of the surplus was enough to purchase other requirements, and make a profit for the county besides. Those forty-one people in that almshouse are no longer paupers, but honorable and valuable residents of the State of Delaware.

There is no reason to doubt that if the same wise methods of giving opportunities to labor and to produce were also given to the inmates of all the almshouses of our land, and of all other lands, all the almshouses would become self-sustaining, and the inmates of such institutions would cease to become paupers, but would, on the contrary, become serviceable members of society.

And if to the people of all countries were given free access to uncultivated lands, poverty would disappear from the civilized world and almshouses and charitable institutions would be things of the past in civilized communities, or would remain only as curios or as monumental relics of a past barbarism.

There surely is a monstrous injustice somewhere in the system that robs man of his natural rights to produce those commodities necessary for his existence; and as man's genius harnesses to his will newly discovered forces of nature and increases the capacity of man to produce, that injustice is intensified when the methods adopted reduce the opportunities of one set of men to produce for themselves.

If poverty and crime are increased as a consequence of man's inventive genius, it must necessarily, then, follow that the man who discovers new forces in nature, and invents appliances by which man's individual power to produce is increased, is a curse to most of his fellow-men, and so, instead of encouraging mechanical invention, it should be discouraged. It is unthinkable, however, that, Franklin, Fulton, Evans, Whitney, Morse, Ericsson, Edison, and men of their character and mental force can be considered otherwise than blessings to their countrymen.

It is not because man's inventive genius has vastly enlarged man's capacity to produce his wants that poverty and crime increase; it is because of bad government. We have entirely too much paternalism in governments.

Man cannot be too free, he cannot indulge in
too much individualism, so long as he respects
another man's rights. Education teaches respect for others' rights; not by artificial laws is
man taught to respect them. No man can
claim as a just right any individual right that
gives him a monopoly of a natural opportunity. That which nature has created without
the aid of man any man has a natural right to,
in common with his fellow-men. When possessing more of such opportunities than he
can make available for his comforts and necessities, he robs his fellow-men when he denies
to them access to that part of a natural opportunity that he cannot himself make use of.

It is the " dog in the manger " that causes
poverty and crime: in his freedom to trade
with his fellow-men, in whatever manner that
those who do the trading may agree upon,
man should be unrestricted. If A is indebted
to B to the amount of twenty-five dollars,
he should not be restricted in his right to pay
that indebtedness by creating a new one. He
should be permitted, if B is willing to take
such payment, to make five or more notes
payable on demand. It is no one's business
but that of A and B. B may owe other
men who will willingly take A's note in payment of his debts, and those to whom B makes
such payments would find their creditors will-

ing to take A's note, and possibly, after a time, A's notes would be returned to him in payment of amounts due A.

These notes of A's could not be thus circulated as a currency, unless those who took them had faith in the integrity and sound business methods of A. When a paternal government prohibits the use of such currency, because of the fear that some innocent or ignorant holder of such notes will possibly be a loser by using such currency, that government stands upon a par in intellectual development with that parent who refuses to take the necessary health-restoring drug into his house because of his fear that some of his innocent and ignorant children will get a part of it and poison themselves. If any set of legislators seriously contemplate formulating laws to prevent fools from doing foolish things, they are themselves the fools against whom such legislation should be aimed.

CHAPTER IV.

From Rome came the jurisprudence that now governs European civilization. The Roman system of jurisprudence was evolved from centuries of experimental efforts of the governing class of the Commonwealth and Empire of Rome to compel the great mass of the producing class there to be human brutes —mere beasts of burden and of toil. And so effectively had the government of Rome formulated and executed laws for that purpose that, when the Empire reached its greatest attainments in wealth and literature, nearly two-thirds of its population were slaves. Rome made no great advance in either the arts or science. She built magnificent palaces, by calling to her aid the skill and genius of Greece, but it was in war and along the avenues of destruction that she became powerful and great. Might was the foundation of Roman jurisprudence. No soldier of Rome and but few of her statesmen ever questioned the right to possess anything that might could command. From such

ethical culture it is not reasonable to assume
that a system of perfect justice could evolve.

Nor did it. To-day the foundation of the
system of justice in every country of civilization is that of might. Not the possession of a
natural opportunity held by any mortal of to-
day, if traced back far enough, will fail to
reveal the blow, the force, and the ruthless
robbery that tore it from the possession of
someone else. And doubtless, if the history
of the possession of such an opportunity be
carried back far enough, it will show that by
the process of violence it had frequently
changed ownership.

A great Latin prince, believing himself, and
also believed by Church and State, to be the
vicar of God on earth, incapable of doing an
injustice, having been forced by scientists,
not the development of Roman culture, to
accept the belief of the rotundity of the globe,
drew a line across the chart of the new continent, the existence of which had but recently
been made known to him; and to his faithful
subject the King of Spain he said: "All that
is north of the line—land, people, and wealth—
I, as the vicar of God, give to you, to do with
as you may, and all to the south of that line I
give to my faithful subject the King of
Portugal."

In this simple transaction of a Pope whose

goodness of heart and nobleness of purpose
are here not questioned, we have a complete
illustration of Latin jurisprudence. If those
kings could possess themselves of those lands,
rob their inhabitants of their wealth, and en-
slave them, they might justly do so, and the
Almighty God would justify, and Latin civilization and jurisprudence would legalize the
transaction. And to-day the foremost nations
of the world recognize the binding force in
law of that division of a continent made by a
man nearly four hundred years ago.

Surely the dead reigns, and the living bow
in obedience to a lump of clay. Fetichism
among savage men is a vice; among the most
learned, most cultivated, and most progressive
nations of the world it is a cardinal virtue.

And why? Because Roman jurisprudence has declared it to be so, and Thomas
Jefferson to have been an anarchistic teacher
when he taught that the earth in its usufruct
belongs to the living, and that the dead should
have no control of it.

Under the Roman system men apparently
recognized no man's rights to anything that
could safely be taken from him. If man was
strong enough to retain what he became possessed of, his right to it was recognized. The
hero of the Romans was not only a robber,
but a fratricide. He taught his subjects the

art of deceit as a necessary method of establishing homes, and the history of the nation that he established is a history of robbery, murder, and licentiousness. Here and there in the history of Rome are presented such characters as Brutus and Lucretia, but they are as oases in the desert.

Is it not time for the people of the present civilization to cease their fetich worship of unnatural things? For ages men have been submitting themselves to horrible torture, mutilating their bodies and dwarfing their intellects to appease the wrath of undiscernible and unknown demons; but those ages of human torture do not prove the existence of the demons. No more do the system of laws of some kinds of civilization—in spite of the indorsement of ages—prove that such laws are founded on justice.

Modern intelligence has eliminated from civilization the worship of snakes, serpents, cats, and other living things. It has destroyed the faith of educated people in demons, witches, and such uncanny creatures. But intelligence has much more to do to remove fetich impediments from the pathways of human progress. So long as the human mind accepts the proposition that because humanity has for ages believed to be true an economic or ethical proposition, and that those many

years of humanity's faith in the correctness of
the proposition is conclusive evidence of its
truth, so long does that human mind need further education and development.

There are certain propositions the truth of
which is so apparent to the human mind that
words cannot be framed to express the ideas
more comprehensively to the mind than by
merely stating the proposition. The geo-
metrical proposition that a straight line is the
shortest distance between two points cannot,
for example, be more clearly elucidated than
by the bare statement that " The shortest distance between two points is a straight line."
Though a volume of thought be devoted to
elucidation, a mind incapable of accepting
that proposition at once, but demanding
further proof of its accuracy, is incapable of
reasoning, and by its fellows such a mind
would be deemed that of an imbecile.

That which man produces without aid from
his fellow-men should be the property of the
man who produces it, is an axiomatic truth;
that man has a right to opportunities to live
upon earth, is equally true. Man is entitled to
possess whatever he may produce, so long as
in the process of production he has not de-
prived his fellow-man of anything that was his
possession. Man cannot rightly take for his
use that which other men possess, unless by

the consent of the possessor, even though he who possessed it acquired it by unjust methods.

No arguments are needed to sustain the truth of these propositions. They are self-evident. Man should not be permitted by his fellow-men, by society, by government to retain possession of anything he was not justly entitled to possess. If it did not belong to the man, and no owner for it could be found, it should become the common property of society. This logical proposition, however, is not sustained by Roman jurisprudence. By that law it remains the private property of the possessor, to be used by him for his private purpose, and for its misuse he is accountable only when complaint is duly and legally made by the real owner of the property.

If anyone will take the trouble to investigate the suit and the decision regarding it handed down by our highest courts of certain people of New York city against the Old Dutch Church, to compel that church to account for the use or misuse of the old shoemaker's cow pasture " down by the Maiden Lane," he will see that the highest courts declare that persons holding illegal possession of property cannot be disturbed in the possession of it, save by complaint of the real owner of it. Fetich worship of Roman jurisprudence makes an anarchist of the man who asserts that property illegally in possession of individuals, and for which real owners cannot be found, should be confiscated for the use of society. " Possession is nine points of the law." Justice may hold one.

When the Great Master went up to Jerusalem preaching a new philosophy, He was denounced both by Church and State as an anarchistic teacher. In the beginning of His work He was simply the despised Nazarene. And the same spirit that disdainfully exclaimed in the last Presidential contest, " What do the hayseeds know of finance?" lived, clothed in purple and fine linen or in sacerdotal robes, in Jerusalem upward of nineteen centuries ago, and disdainfully asked the question, " What good ever came out of Nazareth?" The Master taught a simple philosophy. One so easily comprehended that any mind not indurated by selfish injustice or Roman jurisprudence could comprehend and understand it. The whole philosophy of Christ's teaching was epitomized in His injunction to His followers, " Do unto others as you would have others do unto you." The man who desires special privileges to trade cannot be wise and honest according to the Master's standard.

If wise, he knows full well that he can possess and make use of no special privileges to trade that will admit of him doing " unto others as he would have others do unto him." If he be wise and asks for special privileges, he intends to get more than an equivalent for what he intends to give, as it is his intention that his fellow-men shall, by their necessities, be compelled to give him more than an equivalent for what he gives them. If he be wise, and seeks to possess any of these special privileges, he is not honest if he pretends to Christian virtues. By the standard of Lycurgus he would be honest, provided he could conceal the method by which he got the better of his fellow-men in the deal. By the Roman standard he would be both honest and honored if he could retain possession of what he got, no matter by what means.

But the pretended basis of justice in the United States is Christ's philosophy. Equity is presumably based upon Christ's teachings. The exponents of law to-day should be as wise as those of any preceding period of the world's history. It is even a fair assumption to say that they should be wiser. They know that when the Romans accepted Christianity as a state religion, they modified that religion to accord with Roman thought, to such an ex-

tent as almost to destroy its resemblance to
the religion taught by the Apostles; they know
that Rome accepted Christian precepts. The
Christian nations of to-day, not even excepting those under the full sway of the Roman
Church, no longer teach the religion of Constantine, but that of the Apostles, as the correct foundation for the ethics of our daily lives.
All, however, in their political and economic
systems, cling to the traditions of Constantine
and his successors, as their reverence for the
Justinian code proves.

No better real estate title is held in England
to-day than those of the monastery lands of
that country that Henry VIII., asserting absolutely his own free will, took violent possession
of, and bestowed upon those whom he sought
to reward for personal service. Had Henry
been what he claimed to be,—the personifica-
tion of the people of England,—and taken violent possession of those lands for the benefit of
the whole people of England, there might have
been some justification in the philosophy of
Christ for such confiscation. It is very probable that Henry really believed that all his acts
in that direction, both in the robbery and in
the distribution of the plunder, were for the
best interest of all England. But because he
believed so, and a division of the Christian
Church and the courts of England, as he had

organized them, sustained him in that belief, is no reason why those of the present generation should believe it. He had no more right to limit the freedom of opportunity that those lands afforded—even with the indorsement of every man in England—to the generation that was to follow, than he had to declare that no man born in England after his death should ever wear a coat, or leave the country. Surely it is the dust of the dead that most oppresses mankind, and ancestral worship too greatly prevails in the halls of justice.

An ethical system that turned Europe from an advanced stage of enlightenment into a charnel house of free thought, and plunged it for nearly a thousand years into darkness and decay, from which it was rescued only by external pressure, is a system well worth abandoning; and it would have long since been abandoned had not civilized man been pre-eminently a conservative animal.

Give any man a happy home and ease, and he is likely to rest contented with what he has, and frown upon any proposition that may disturb his enjoyments. That is the artificial man. Most civilized men's natures are artificial—the creation of their environments. So long has man been oppressed by tradition that most men easily learn even to question the proposition that they have a right to live;

they readily accept the belief that they can only live by the consent of the divinely anointed, or heavenly appointed of their fellows. When a happy home and an easy existence become his share of this world's gifts, man is too anxious to retain them to consent to any radical departure from the traditions of the fathers, from whom he believes he may have become possessed of those good things. Hence it follows that no radical reformation of economic systems may be expected to originate or be effected by those who possess the wealth of the country. Selfishness, contentment, and ignorance—allies in the maintenance of governmental monopolies—have rarely failed to maintain their supremacy. The most powerful factor for evil in this alliance is that of ignorance. It can generally be depended upon as an all-powerful reserve. The " men who think that they think " are perhaps the most dangerous of the ignorant class. This class is largely composed of well-dressed, well-preserved men, who know something of the art of making money and of polite society, who consider it rather vulgar to be in " politics," whose reading of political literature is restricted to the limits of a very partisan but eminently refined newspaper, the tone of which harmonizes with what they believe to be their own really intelligent political convictions, but which more nearly resemble a fetichism.

To many such men gold and silver are money, whether in the form of bullion or of coin. They believe that, in the limitless ages that have passed, God made those metals that man might have money. Some of this class of men who "thought that they thought" have had a hard rap on their brains in the last twenty years by the odd freaks in which silver has been indulging; and they are becoming a little skeptical of the theory that God made silver for man's money; and by this skepticism many minds may become emancipated from the fetichism that gold and silver are natural money.

A worthy gentleman, twice elected by a most complimentary vote Governor of one of the Pacific States, wrote, a few years ago, for one of the popular monthlies, an article on money, in which, with apparent seriousness, he set forth the proposition that the failure of the gold and silver supply began in the third or fourth century of the Christian era, and, continuing until a beneficent providence most mercifully guided Columbus to the New World and new supplies, was the real cause of the decadence of Europe during those centuries. And the discovery of vast deposits of silver and gold in accessible places in

America was, he said, the cause of the rapid intellectual development of Europe during the last four centuries.

Was that Governor a wise man, or should he be classed among the ignorant allies who so valiantly and, alas! so successfully support governmental monopolies? Evidently this man had no intelligent conception of the greatness of the Venetian republic, nor knew anything of the mighty commerce and trade promoted by the Bank of Venice without the assistance of an ounce of gold or silver money; promoted simply on the basis of the credit that men might inspire who possess honesty, good business methods, with other forms of wealth, other than that of gold or silver money; a banking system in which honesty, sobriety, industry, and business capabilities were more desirable securities than gold or silver.

CHAPTER V.

THE use of money became a necessity to man when, in his onward progress, he passed beyond a certain stage of barbarism into the limits of civilization. And in like manner did textile fabrics. Gold and silver were made use of for the purpose of expediting exchanges, and became money, or rather that portion of those metals became money that was made use of solely for purposes of expediting exchange.

But textile fabrics, in certain countries and at certain stages of civilization, were also used for the purpose of expediting exchanges, and that part of such textile fabrics used for that purpose became money. As money they were also commodities.

Gold, silver, and textile fabrics were all commodities. The eternal ages cannot change them from their position as commodities; although it is possible that all of them may cease to be used as money, or as the basis of money. They would never have been used as money had they possessed no commodity value. They would not have been used as money if the use of them as money had destroyed their commodity value. Their value as money was only at par with their commodity value.

Gold and silver money must be in the future what it has always been in the past—commodities only. Money made from those metals or from any other metal is now, always has been, and always will be, considered by commercial operators as commodities. Their value is not ascertained by the ciphers stamped upon them, but by weight, and by the assayer.

By the Bank of England the value of a deposit of gold sovereigns is not determined by counting, but by weighing. Surely, at the Bank of England the gold sovereign is not considered as money. A like weight of gold bars of the same fineness, and coined gold sovereigns are accepted for exactly the same value by that Bank. The fact that a pound of gold has been coined by the authority of England adds nothing to its bullion value. The notes of the Bank of England might be termed money, but not commodity, if they were not exchangeable at the will of the holder into gold or other commodities of equal value. This exchangeability of the notes of the Bank of England makes commodities of them as absolutely as the articles that they buy are commodities, and so must all other governmental or private bills issued for the purpose of money be classed as commodities. They who exchange cloth for Bank of England notes buy those notes. Money is as much a commodity as is the article it buys. If the dealers in money be put in possession of power to control the issue of money, they possess a power to oppress the users of money that should not be given to them. As long as the money-dealers possess this power—to a limited or an unlimited extent—they create in the popular mind a distrust that any unusual commercial disorder is almost sure to intensify. As the basis of the world's money is gold, a commercial disturbance of any great magnitude in any part of the world creates, among all the people of the commercial world, distrust in their ability to exchange the products of their labor for an amount of money that will compensate them for the cost of production.

This distrust is at once an incentive for those who have money convertible at their option into gold, to hoard their money, which at once creates a scarcity of it and a greater disturbance of business. Gold, being a basis of money that has already been hoarded, is, for the purposes of its daily business, practically useless to the commercial world. If the monetary system be inflexible,—and that is practically the case with the world's money at the present time,—those who possess great wealth immediately proceed to conserve their holdings at all times of business disturbances, by drawing their lines of ventures to the safest possible contraction. The first called upon to liquidate their indebtedness are the weaker members of the business men of the country, the ones who really need and should have the greatest support. The money-dealers at such times are critical about the character of their credits, and seek to reduce the limit of that credit to circles where their personal knowledge may better serve the safety of their investments. Money-dealers, as a class, live in the great money business-centers in the great cities; and it is but natural that they should limit their lines of credit on occasions of commercial disturbances to the vicinity of their home city. The weaker communities are as much depressed and disturbed by the business disturbance that was the primary cause of the distrust, as the wealthy communities are, and, in addition to this general disturbance, a demand is made upon them to pay at once, or at short time, obligations that they would not have been called upon to pay, and were not expected to pay, until a much later date; but would have had simply to pay interest thereon.

This power of the money-lender, without any sordid or selfish motive on the part of but few of them,—strictly· following a necessity of business only, or what they are justified in esteeming a business necessity,—has had more to do, during the past fifty years, with building up great cities and with prostrating small communities than any other one economic factor has had.

When a government, by the exercise of the natural rights of its people, institutes a monetary system that prevents any substitute for money, it institutes a monetary system that is absolutely inflexible. If there is any one feature of the money question that bankers, financiers, and business men do agree upon, it is that a currency system to be perfect must provide for a flexible currency; a currency that, in regard to quantity, will adjust itself to the requirements of the various communities of that country.

Many of our serious statesmen, who have been chosen by their fellow-men to legislate for them in Congress, have been enervating their mental forces by attempting to formulate a monetary system by which the Government should supply sufficiently large paper issues of money to preclude the possibility of any in-

dustrial section of the country from ever being
without a sufficient supply of currency. But
so long as they confine their efforts to a system that provides for confining the issuing of
paper money exclusively to the Government,
or to government control, they seek after the
unattainable. It would be fully as wise, if not
wiser, were they to devote their mental forces
to devise some plan by which the Government could control the output of wheat,
corn, cotton, and other commodities quite as
important in commercial and industrial enterprises as money. They would succeed in establishing a more perfect plan of promoting
the happiness of the whole people, if they
could formulate laws that would compel every
man to do his share of the labor of producing
those commodities necessary to the comfort
and happiness of the people of our country,
and secure to each man a just reward for his
labor.

To provide a satisfactory currency exclusively by governmental issue, that will adjust itself to the requirement of all parts of the
country at all times, is far more difficult than
that of controlling the productions of commodities or to control the energy of the country. No sane man would propose that a
government should control energy or the production of commodities, and it is difficult to

determine why any sane man should advocate the control, by the Government, of the volume of currency to be used. The function of government should be limited to coining a standard by which exchange may be expedited, to fix a standard of weight by which certain commodities may expeditiously be exchanged for others, and to establish a standard of measures for the convenience of trading in such commodities that custom and convenience may demand.

Why should the Government control the quality and quantity of currency-issue any more than it should control the quality and quantity of cotton produced? Men may be deceived into buying worthless cotton as readily as they may be deceived into buying worthless currency. They honestly get possession of each only by purchase or production. Education and the police powers of government, rightly directed, are capable of preventing serious disasters from afflicting the public from deceit, either from the owners of worthless currency or worthless cotton.

Three great political parties of the United States held conventions in 1896, to formulate political principles and to nominate candidates for President and Vice President. The first convention to assemble, that of the Republican party, declared, " All our silver and paper

money must be maintained at parity with gold,
and we favor all measures designed to maintain inviolable the obligations of the United
States and all our money, whether coin or
paper money, at the present standard—the
standard of the most enlightened nations of
the world."

This was a prettily worded resolution, and
was quite as sensible as another would have
been that had been made to read that, "All
the wheat, corn, and oats grown in the United
States must be equal in quality to the best
grown anywhere else in the world, and we
pledge the solemn obligations of the United
States that no man shall be permitted to grow,
buy, or sell, a bushel of wheat, corn, or oats
that is not equal in quality to the best of these
grains produced anywhere in the world."

The Democratic convention, which met a
month later in Chicago, "demanded free and
unlimited coinage of gold and silver at a ratio
of 1 to 16." This might have been a proper
demand in 1872, but in 1896, if such a demand
could have been enforced, owing to the
changed conditions of trade in the world, its
enforcement would have so seriously disturbed
the industries of the country that it is beyond
man to calculate the calamity that might have
resulted as a consequence. That the bullion
value of silver would have advanced under the

action of free coinage of silver by the United States, scarcely admits of a doubt, and it is equally certain that the purchasing power of gold would have been depreciated; but that they would have finally settled to a point where the ratio of the two metals would have been 1 to 16, can scarcely be considered even as a possibility. The result would have been that we would have had two standards: that of gold, which would be the standard of measuring the value of all commodities we import, and that of silver, for measuring the values of all commodities we produce.

Labor's reward, after a period of readjustment, would probably not be much affected by a double standard. The wages of the laborer under either system would purchase like quantities of commodities. Labor gets no more or less commodities than labor can command. The wages of labor is ultimately labor's products. Labor that commands the amount of labor's products that an ounce of gold will buy, will not be contented with only the amount of labor's products that sixteen ounces of silver will buy.

A change from the gold to the silver standard in the United States will not Mexicanize the American laborer. It is well known that employers of labor do not reward their employees from a sense of gratitude or from human sympathy, but simply on the purely business principle of the cheapest markets. They will pay as little as they are compelled to, and they will employ labor only so long as they believe it profitable.

Under the system of human justice prevailing throughout the civilized world, members of what is known as the laboring class are compelled to a very great extent to accept those wages that will give them a barely comfortable existence, because of the great competition among them for the privilege of living.

The laborers of this country, especially in the agrarian districts, are now about in that condition, that they cannot take less wages and live. They still have remaining some unmonopolized opportunities. They can fish in the streams, hunt on the marshes and on the hills, and little patches of land are generally accessible to them. And when wages fall to a point where by fishing, hunting, and hoeing a man can make a more comfortable existence than by wage-earning in factories, thousands avail themselves of the few remaining free opportunities to work for themselves. Labor supply, then, becomes scarce, and employers of labor are compelled to pay increased wages.

In countries where every opportunity to live

is denied to man, save by special privilege from a few individuals, men can be compelled to labor their weary lives through for sufficient rice and bread for maintaining a miserable existence; but not so, yet, in the United States, nor even in Mexico. Nor would wages in Mexico be so low as they are if man's necessities there were greater. If there were less sun and fewer bananas, and more frost and grass in Mexico, wages there would be higher per capita. Measured by the work performed, there are but few places in the world where labor is so well rewarded as in Mexico.

The exact meaning of the language used in the plank of the Chicago platform of 1896 that relates to the currency bills was not very clear, excepting so far as it related to the national bank system. There was no mistaking that the Democratic party, of which the Chicago convention was the oracle, demanded that "the right to issue paper money should not be delegated by the Government of the United States to corporations or to individuals." It did not demand that paper money should be issued by the Government, nor did it advocate nor oppose the giving to corporations or to individuals the right to issue bills that might be used for currency.

But it did most emphatically protest against the Government conferring legal-tender privileges upon any currency not issued by the Government.

It is a fair inference, however, that the Chicago platform of 1896 advocated the issuing, by the Government, of paper money armed with legal-tender powers and redeemable in coin, either of gold or silver, at the option of the Government.

Few men will dispute the correctness of the theory that the Government should not confer legal-tender powers upon currency issued otherwise than by the Government itself. The only essential difference between the Republican and the Chicago platform, so far as they relate to the currency question, is that the Republicans demanded that all paper money issued by the Government shall be redeemable in gold, while the Chicago platform demanded that such notes must be redeemed in coin.

It is evident that the majority of the American voters believed that, when the Government opened its mints to the free coinage of silver, silver would displace gold as the basis of the American paper dollar, and that the dollar bill would be redeemable in a coin the gold value of which would be considerably less than that of a gold dollar. And they also believed that such was the true meaning of the currency plank of the Chicago platform.

It is equally evident, on the other hand,

that the majority of voters believed that the election of Mr. McKinley insured the redemption in gold of every bill issued or guaranteed by the Government.

The Republican party is pledged to continue the Government in the banking business. Whether by bond-selling or increased taxation, it is pledged to maintain a sufficient amount of gold in the Treasury to maintain the public confidence. This is embodied in the declaration that, " All our silver and paper money must be maintained at parity with gold." It practically stamps silver as a base metal, and the silver dollar as a fiat dollar.

Would it not have been greater wisdom had the Republican party declared that silver was too valuable a metal to be used as tokens for money? that paper was less expensive and more convenient for that purpose? that good business principles demand that the silver dollar, together with the silver bullion not necessary for subsidiary currency now in the Treasury of the United States, should be sold in the best attainable markets? and paper money, to the value realized from such sales of silver, should be issued instead? or, at least, such amount of it as the business of the country demanded? This would have been a more logical declaration to make.

If the silver dollar is a fiat dollar, and,

surely, under the present monetary system of
the United States, no one will seriously claim
that it is not, why should the Government pay
fifty cents' worth of gold for a piece of silver
upon which to stamp "one dollar," when for
that amount of gold enough paper may be
bought to make, perhaps, five hundred one-
dollar notes. Certainly no one who uses
money in the United States will give more
commodities or more labor for a silver dollar
than he would give for a paper dollar. Outside of the United States, among civilized
people, the paper dollar will command the
greater price, because it will cost less to get it
back to its highest market.

The National Democracy, that assembled
in convention at Indianapolis, declared, with
an emphasis that cannot be misunder-
stood, against a continuance of the "present patchwork system" of national paper
currency, and maintained the necessity of
such intelligent currency reforms as will
confine the Government to its legitimate
functions, completely separate it from banking business, "and afford to all sections
of our country a uniform, safe, and elastic currency under governmental supervision, measured in volume by the needs of the country."

That this plank of the Indianapolis platform clearly stated the necessities of currency

reform, cannot be disputed. That it acknowl-
edged the urgent necessity of an elastic currency is apparent also. But, unfortunately,
the way to accomplish this necessary reform,
and thus secure the elastic currency acknowl-
edged to be a necessity, is but opaquely inti-
mated. The Government supervisors capable
of measuring the needs for currency of the
various parts of the United States and the extent of the volume best suited to such needs,
as well as the methods of getting the currency
to them, are angels that have not yet been
sent to earth. And if the people are compelled to await their coming before such
monetary reform can be instituted, it is useless to waste further time and thought on the
subject.

The Government should retire from banking business entirely. So long as it issues
paper money, or controls its issue, or guarantees the face value of bills or of anything else
issued as a substitute for money, it remains in
the banking business. To explain how the
Government can separate itself entirely from
the banking business, yet supervise the banking business at one and the same time, must
be left to those gentlemen who are responsible
for that Indianapolis currency plank. The
Government's business with the money of the
country is to stamp a measure of value on

"coin money." There its obligation to the
people ends. To do more than that for many
years of the country's history has generally
been believed to be an usurpation of power
not delegated to it by the States. The Government should demand from its citizens that
taxes should be paid with the standard. And
it, too, should pay its debts with the standard
coins and thus let the citizens be free, each
State, each community ascertaining the means
of expediting its business, and in such a manner as it is believed is best suited to promote
its greatest interests.

The impetus that the possessors of good
character, correct business methods, and
wealth may give to industrial developments of communities has emphatically been
shown in an illustrious example—the Bank of
Venice. For upward of six hundred years
that bank, notwithstanding revolutions, the
wreck of empires, and the unceasing geographical changes, practically sustained the
enormous commerce of the Adriatic and the
Black seas, and their thousands of miles of
tributary rivers—a most gigantic force in the
intellectual development of Europe; a force,
too, that destroyed the charnel house of
free thought that Roman jurisprudence and
religion had for so many centuries maintained.
It was this commerce, promoted by the **Bank**

of Venice, that made a Galileo and a Columbus possibilities in Rome. A Church that had accepted the belief that the earth was a flat disk, surrounded by impassable walls and held in position by four enormous elephants,— without troubling itself to explain what power sustained the elephants,—and a judiciary that sanctioned the Church's prosecution of Hypatia because she taught that such a proposition was absurd, was not likely to develop scientists and navigators. It was intercourse with people who had read the stars and studied natural developments of animal and plant life, and wanted to know some reason for the cause that produced the effects other than that it was the will of an unknown personality. The fact that the vicar, in Rome, of that unknown personality was often a very bad man, made progressive Romans susceptible students of the Alexandrian schools. Commerce on those seas and on their tributary rivers was, to the Middle Ages, what the trackless waters of the ocean are to commerce of the world to-day.

The Bank of Venice did not deal in money; did not receive it on deposit; did not pay it out on drafts; it was simply a clearing house of commodities and credits. Of course the measure of values by which exchange of commodities was expedited was gold and silver.

Men well known to the management of the Bank for their business ability, integrity, and worth, lent to the bank their indorsement to a limited amount, and on the basis of such loans the Bank issued trading certificates or letters of credit, so much more valuable to the commercial venturers of that period of political disturbance than was either gold or silver, that users of these certificates were frequently willing to pay a premium above the value of gold for the privilege; and, at times, upward of thirty per cent. was paid as premiums. The system of the Bank of Venice was simply that of bookkeeping. The Bank continued to do business—a mighty factor in promoting commercial and industrial developments in Venice—until that ruthless destroyer of industrial development, the great Napoleon, overthrew it by war and devastation.

The history of the building of a market house on the little island of Guernsey is a good illustration of what can be done without money of gold or silver—or any form of money the soundness of which was guaranteed by a great government. One of the towns of that island felt the need of a market house, but it could not raise the money necessary to build it. It was ascertained that there was an abundance of material, enough skilled and unskilled artisans accessible that money could readily command. The governor of the island, Daniel DeLisle Brock, determined that the market house should be built; that the skill and material were accessible; money was not a necessity. He issued five thousand one-pound notes. To inspire confidence in owners of the material needed for the building, and in the artisans necessary for its erection, he made those notes legal tenders on the island of Guernsey. But making them legal tenders did not inspire as much confidence in the value of those notes as was inspired by the character of the people who issued them. Every man who received those notes believed that they would be redeemed in the best and most precious money of England, or its equivalent in other commodities.

Legal-tender notes are by no means always accepted at their face value in standard money, save by those who are compelled by law so to accept. And by the nation that issues them they are maintained at par with the standard only at great cost. Competent financiers maintain, with great force, that it has cost the United States upward of two billions of dollars to maintain the greenback currency at par with gold.

The community of St. Peters accepted these notes issued by Governor Brock, it being clearly understood that the notes were only to

be issued to pay for the construction of the
market house; the notes were to be returned
to the governor for rentals of that house, and
when returned were not to be reissued save
for repairs or work upon the market house.
And as these notes from time to time accumulated, beyond the amount necessary for construction and repairs to the house, they were
destroyed by the governor. In the course of
a very few years all these notes were collected
by Governor Brock; and by him, in the presence of the assembled people of the town, they
were canceled by flame. There in a remote
island of England, by a people in affinity more
French than English, a most excellent market
house was built, which for many years served
as a useful building and a source of income to
the people of St. Peters; and without a coin
of the Government or a note of governmental
creation. What was done in the town of St.
Peters on the Isle of Guernsey may be done
anywhere else on earth, when the material and
the labor are accessible, without the aid of
anything that the majority of sound-money
economists term money.

To say it is possible that Governor Brock's
system may be useful in small communities,
but not in great nations, is to advance a
convincing argument against extending to
the central government the control of

monetary systems. If a great government cannot insure as much happiness and as comfortable an existence to its people as a government of a small community can, there is then no questioning of the fact that a great government is to its people an affliction rather than a blessing, and that any effort by anyone to extend the boundaries of a nation is in the direction of a further oppression of the people of that nation.

Some such thought undoubtedly pervaded the minds of our Revolutionary fathers. The fear of centralizing the powers of the Government seems to have possessed the minds of all who had fought for liberty during the period between the acknowledgment of American Independence and the adoption of the Federal Constitution. And, apparently, it was a great relief to all when plans of the Government were adopted that gave to the Central Government the dignity of a great nation, with powers to maintain that dignity before the world, yet, at the same time, giving to each State of the Union the privilege of self-government. United for protection against external aggression, they divided for internal progress. Hence a community of free States, throughout which freedom to trade was the equal right of all its citizens, and where personal privileges and individual freedom were granted to

or taken from them by the authority of the
State only; that is, only to the very limited
extent to which the authority of the United
States had been restricted by the States upon
the adoption of the Federal Constitution.

In the United States the man who robs cannot be punished by the laws of the United
States, save in the few cases where the power
to punish criminals has been conceded by the
States to the general Government. Man is
practically protected in his property and personal rights by the laws of the States, and the
national Government, without usurpation of
authority, cannot punish. The Federal Government can punish for illicit distilling of
spirits, for smuggling, for counterfeiting
National Government, without usurpation of
such acts as are unlawful under Federal
statutes, provided those Federal statutes do
not usurp the privilege or right of the States.
But there the Federal powers to punish
crimes in the United States end.

Has this feature of the Federal Government
been its weakness or its strength during the
past eleven decades of its existence?

Is there a student of politics and of history
in all the wide world, who has a reputation
worth considering, who will have the hardi-
hood to write above his signature the
declaration that he believes the United States

would have been more progressive and have grown to greater eminence in arts, science, justice, and power, had a monarchy—no matter what kind, from the autocracy of Russia to the freedom of England—been erected here in 1788 instead of a Republic of republics?

There is no reason to doubt that men can be made happier by self-government than by dictatorial government. There is no doubt but that climatic conditions affect man's natural tastes and sensibilities; there is no doubt that a system of government may be perfectly acceptable to New York and much esteemed there, and believed to be nearly or quite a perfect system, which in other parts of the country would be perfectly worthless, while in still other parts it would be even harmful.

These are plain common-sense propositions that demand the thoughtful attention of the American people; and until they are given serious attention there can be no greatly beneficial reforms in the monetary system of the country. Bimetallism would practically aid monetary reform, if it could be successfully accomplished. But it could be successfully accomplished only by the united effort of the commercial nations of the world. Government issue of all the paper money permitted to be used in the country would not be a reform; it would be a decided retrogression.

No kind of paper money can be made a legal tender for debts and be of advantage to the people of the country that issues it. It will, however, prove to be of immense advantage to some people of those countries who deal in money. Fiat money is fruitful money to the money-dealers and money-changers.

CHAPTER VI.

It is a serious study to determine what kind of currency a sound financial policy demands for business purposes; to make such currency the best attainable money possible, or, in other words, to make it not only sound currency but one also readily available for currency purposes in all communities equitably entitled to it. That there has never been a very clear definition of what the term " sound currency " is intended to imply, is much to be regretted. If it is to be read as meaning a currency to be used only for the payment of interest and taxes, the soundest currency, then, would undoubtedly be the currency that could be most readily disposed of in exchange for commodities in any of the markets of the world. It is, therefore, unnecessary to say that such a currency should be made of gold.

Inasmuch as the commercial industry and enterprise of the British kingdom have best acquainted the commercial world with the gold sovereign of England, that coin would perhaps suit best for an international or an all-round trading currency. But to use the British gold currency in the United States would be a source of much inconvenience, and, if used here, doubtless would in many cases be to the disadvantage of many ill-informed people.

If this proposition be correct, it follows, then, that no gold coin or any coin whatever can be the best currency, even if it be sound currency like the British sovereign or the American gold dollar. All there is of value in coin-money, not possessed by any other kind of money, is the bullion value of such coin as a measure.

To enter into an argument to prove this proposition is unnecessary. The commerce of the world proves it. The ratio of coin-payment to the total payment of commercial and State obligations is so infinitesimally small it is scarcely to be represented in figures. So long as the great trading nations of the world use gold bullion as a measure to effect exchanges and settle balances, there can be no currency sounder than a currency of gold coins of fixed and reliable weight and fineness. Such coins are rarely used for currency; they are used rather as a measure of value.

Even in France, where small silver coins are so generally used by the people, paper currency circulates to many times the value of the coin in use. Paper is used there almost exclusively for currency, except where fractional currency is necessary; even the subsidiary silver coins are banked away by the thrifty French peasantry for safe-keeping. It is true that France in her financial system makes use of nearly or quite $1,200,000,000 worth of gold and silver coin. But $750,000,-000 worth of paper money furnishes the working medium of exchange for her tradesmen; and at least three-quarters of her coin is held in reserve for what is believed to be necessary for the maintenance of a sound business and financial system. It is not used to perform the functions of money any more than gold and silver bars, the weight and fineness of which are vouched for by the Government, would perform such functions.

The United States held in its vaults, January 1, 1895, nearly $650,000,000 in gold and silver coins and bullion; and nearly $500,000,-000 more was held by banking institutions and individuals in safe-deposit vaults. The value of coins circulating as currency among the people certainly would not be any larger than that represented by the silver dollars and subsidiary coins—nearly all silver—reported by the Treasury Department to have been taken out of the Mint, the coin value of which was stated to have been $120,561,176. The paper money in circulation at the same time was also reported to have been upward of $1,000,000,000.

There can be no disputing the fact that all of the United States silver money is worth, as money, nearly or quite double the amount it is worth as bullion.   Fifty per cent. of its money value is simply the result of a fiat of the Government; and therefore it should be properly classed with paper money—of a better grade, perhaps.   Both silver and paper money are freely accepted by the people of the United States as money, owing to the faith of the people in the intention and ability of the maker of such money to keep its face value in parity with the soundest money of the world—gold. The assurance of its weight and fineness is stamped upon it by a Government commanding the confidence of the commercial world; and, so stamped, without any regard to a ratio between gold and silver bullion, it is just such stamping as England puts upon her gold money.   That the legal-tender quality of this money would force the people to take it unwillingly, is true.

Great Britain, to keep her gold coin in the country, does not permit an issuance, in England proper, of paper bills of less value than one-pound denomination.   The Bank of England issues none for less than five pounds.   Consequently, in England's home business, a far greater proportion of coined money to paper is issued than elsewhere among the great commercial nations of the world. This, however, does not prove that the masses in England are made richer thereby. The compactness of the English people doubtless enables their business to be conducted with less currency than other nations of like business volume, whose people are scattered over a many-times greater area. England requires but $600,000,000 worth of coin and bills to transact all her enormous business, while France needs three times that amount. Germany uses nearly $1,500,000,000 worth of currency in various forms, and the United States has more than $2,000,000,000, and, from intelligent sources from all parts of the country, the demand upon the Government is made for more.

This demand for more currency invites the most serious attention of every American citizen. This request does not come from silver-producing States alone, nor can it be lightly pushed aside as we would push the demands of thoughtless children, consoling ourselves with the belief that we are wiser than they, and know better their needs. When such States as Kansas request, in unlimited quantities, free coinage of silver, we cannot, as wise men, deny that request on the assumption that her population is too ignorant to be permitted to influence financial legislation. Kansas was settled by the best blood of New England. Her schoolhouses and churches were built while yet the floor-beams of her homesteads were being laid. A newspaper was an established fact before the teacher and the preacher had been assigned to duty there. Such was the method of settling Kansas, and in her moral and intellectual development she has taken no steps backward.

In the demand made by Kansas and other States where there can be no such influence as silver mines and silver-mine boomers to influence the votes of the people, it is plainly to be seen that there is in the currency system an inequality, an injustice, and a disturbing influence great enough to fill the minds of the leading men of highly intelligent communities with a desire for some radical change in the money system. The gold coins, they know by experience, cannot keep in circulation, and by sad experience they also know that the paper money, circulating upon the faith in the Government and upon a gold basis, is also, on the least disturbance in the money market, taken from them to the great money centers. When needed most, it is to be had only by the weaker communities making business-destroying sacrifices of their commodities.

It is the hope, possibly, that a money made

of or based upon silver, which would not be so easily attracted from them, that impelled them so urgently to demand unlimited silver and free coinage. That silver money would act differently with them than gold acts now is not probable. It is not gold or silver that they so much demand; it is some form of currency that will expedite business transactions. They know the present system is dangerously faulty; they believe, in fact, it could not be worse; that any change would be an improvement. Upon free coinage of silver they compromised, because it was to them apparently a possibility, and was a radical measure. Few people, however studious, who have not had intimate relations with the country districts of the United States, can begin to realize how great is the volume of business done in many country districts of the United States simply by barter.

This demand for money, made by so many of the States, is not altogether the demand of ignorance. Governmental policies have always been more or less speculative, and that there is much of the speculative in the theory of free coinage of silver is indeed true. The business men of the South and West want a more convenient medium of exchange than they now have. The national banking system has failed to provide currency, with equity and justice, to the entire people.

Rather, indeed, has that system enabled the banking institutions of the great commercial centers to control at times the volume of circulation of currency notes. In most cases, it is true, they have done this for their own protection, or rather for the protection of the industries that their particular banking system largely sustained. On such occasions they have oppressed the commercial industries of other centers—in many cases to the extent even of destroying them.

The people of the South and West have for years in their business relations been subjected to conditions that have made it exceedingly difficult for them to transact business. Those having the strongest—financially considered—Eastern connection possessed advantages. The weaker sections, however, could not transact their usual business with that freedom from friction that in the more favored parts of the country was usual, owing to the scarcity of currency notes. Small checks, common in the West, particularly with tradesmen, were used frequently as currency, which after many months came back to the bank on which they were drawn, soiled and covered with indorsements. No other proof is needed to show that more currency was required in such communities, and that a currency as sound as the gold dollar was not the best currency for expediting the business of such communities. It is absurd to say that, if the people of the West have commodities worth the amount of currency they desire, they can demand the currency bills. Such is not the fact. In every case where his checks were used for currency, not only did the maker possess the commodities to the full extent of the face value of that check, but he had also put those commodities into the most convenient form for exchange into currency bills. By the usual process, he had established a credit at his bank by exchanging his commodities for that bank's indorsement or credit. But experience had taught him that such credit would permit him to use, in a more or less cumbersome way, the bank's credit and his own in the character of a check to liquidate his own indebtedness to the extent of the credit established, but would not give him circulating bills.

This proposition should be clearly understood. He established a credit at that bank by making a deposit that was accepted by the management of the bank as equal in value to gold dollars—to the extent represented on the book of the bank's deposits. If the currency system in use in our country had been the best, the man who deposited his funds in the national bank, " Bar-

ren Lands," Idaho, should have no more difficulty to draw out his money in greenbacks or
national-bank bills, or even gold, than has the
merchant who banks in the Chemical Bank of
New York. So long as such bills may more
readily be secured from the banks of New
York than from the banks of St. Paul, then
New York has an advantage over St. Paul
sufficient to justify the people of St. Paul in
demanding of the Government a different
condition. This is true so long as the Government assumes parental control over the
banking interests of the country.

To dwell a little while on the present system of barter prevailing in the South and
West may not be a waste of time. The country merchants in the Southern and Western
States are practically the people's bankers.
But the people in those sections of the country
make deposits with their bankers, not in
money, but in commodities, and receive payment, not in money, but in commodities. The
condition of such a banking system is that the
merchant will receive one kind of commodity
on deposit, and will pay out in the same or in
another kind of commodity, but make payments in commodities only. In many communities throughout the South and West
money is almost an unknown article. No one
of sense will claim that such a condition

represents a healthy business in those communities.

The farmer takes his eggs, butter, corn, wheat, poultry, etc., to the merchant. In almost all sections of the country, eggs are readily accepted, and at all times, by the merchant, at prices fixed from day to day by him; but with nearly all other commodities the purchaser of them must consult the merchant before bringing them to him for deposit or sale, as it may not be convenient for him to take the commodities at that particular time. This, of itself, is a great inconvenience to the producer. Nor can the merchant, in safety to his own interest, do otherwise—else doubtless he would; for it is to the interest of the merchant to be popular; and self-interest would prompt him to accept all commodities offered by the producer at an agreed price, and at any time, were not such commodities presented to him as would make it unsafe for him to do so. Eggs furnish to a very great extent a subsidiary currency to the country people. This the following incidents show:

On one occasion, in a country store in Maryland, a lad came and ordered a dozen grains of quinine, in payment of which he handed up to the clerk two eggs. It seemed to be no unusual transaction either to the boy or the druggist. On another occasion, in

the same State, a New York lad, temporarily
on a visit to his uncle, a storekeeper, was behind the counter of that uncle's store when an
old colored woman passed up to him an egg
with the request to give her " a roll of pins
and de balance in snuff."

When trade-conditions in those country districts are so good that the country merchants
are always ready to buy any of the farmer's
products, the farmer frequently establishes a
credit at the merchant's. His deposits of
commodities may exceed his withdrawals of
commodities, perhaps, by several hundred
dollars' worth, but he ...n close the account
only by withdrawing commodities to the value
of the balance. In such cases the country
producer pays his own indebtedness by giving orders to those whom he wishes to pay
and who will receive such orders on the merchants. But it is always understood that
such orders or drafts are to paid in commodities. The merchant sends his eggs,
poultry, and grain to the cities, to be sold on
his account. In return for his products,
checks are sent, which go directly or indirectly
to the city merchant from whom he makes
his purchases. In many such communities a
country merchant who sells $50,000 worth of
goods in a year has often not handled, in that
time, $5000 worth of money. Indeed, there

are communities of producers who have produced $100,000 worth of commodities for sale,
of which $99,000 has been bartered. It is in
such communities, and where such conditions
exist, that free-coinage advocates are most
numerous, and where converts to such a
speculative theory of finances are easily' made.
It is in such communities that " Coin's Financial School " found attentive pupils.

If we may hope to turn such communities
from the worship of the silver idol, we must
offer them a currency that their commodities
will command, and that the bank there will
be abundantly able, on all conditions of honest and healthy business, to supply to their
depositors; the dollar, in such communities,
being equal to the best dollar of the country,
and readily exchangeable on demand for the
best dollar in the world, namely, a gold dollar
of the United States. But it need not be of
such a character that a hundred miles away it
will be worth as much as it is in the community
in which the bank that issued it is situated.
For this convenience that bank was created.
If it be possible to create a currency note that
will serve all the purposes of a gold coin of
like stamped value, in a community in which
and for which it was issued, serving all the
purposes in that community that a gold coin
would, and that, at the same time, will be too

unattractive to be diverted from the community for whose convenience it was issued, that, then, would be the best possible currency for that community.

No banker or borrower of money will at this date pretend to assert that the First National Bank of New York is any more beneficial to the people of that city than is the Manhattan Comp~ny Bank, merely because the First National Bank is operated under a national charter, while the Manhattan is under a State charter. And while such an object-lesson exists, it is obviously absurd to claim that the only safe banking system must necessarily be a national system. It is indeed true that national currency and national-bank notes have given the public a most convenient currency with which to travel, but not more so than that possessed by the English people, whose banks are all private corporations, and where the Government is not responsible for the payment of the notes.

The usefulness of the national bank has been much overestimated, while its bad features have not been well understood. To the national banks a monopoly was given when they were first established—and intentionally so. Those national banks organized in 1863 and 1864, which, also, were not dragooned into organizing under a national charter, were so

organized in consequence of a stimulus, the
substance of which was monopoly. The
weaker State-banks were dragooned into
organizing themselves into national banks because of the necessity either to abandon business or to adopt the new national-bank system.
In New York, as well as in several other
States, the bonds held as security by the State
for redemption of circulating notes were quite
as valuable as the United States bonds.
When the Government, in 1865, taxed the
State-bank notes ten per cent. per annum, it
became absolutely necessary that those banks
that could not withdraw their circulating notes
without selling their security bonds should
sell them at once. And they did so. By
those banks loans were called in, payments
demanded, their circulating notes canceled,
and their security bonds redeemed with as
much alacrity as possible, so that, by organizing under the national banking system, those
bonds might be sold to secure money with
which to buy the Government bonds necessary
to place those banks in the condition to save
their already-organized banking business.
Many banks throughout the country were
rich enough to protect themselves against being forced into that national banking system.
They simply called in their circulating notes,
and continued banking business under their

State charter.   And it is a significant fact that
among the banks that to-day have most completely the public confidence, are those State
banks that refused the Government's bribe in
1863-64, and declined to be dragooned into
the national banking system in 1865.

The originators of the national banking
system in 1863 had too vividly before them
the verdict of the people against a really individual national bank, and it was therefore
necessary that they should formulate some
plan of banking other than that which the
people, under the leadership of Jackson and
Benton, had buried beyond resurrection more
than twenty-five years before. And the
national banking system adopted by Secretary
Chase, Jay Cooke, E. G. Spaulding, and other
brilliant financiers of that day, was a system
that only geniuses of the highest order could
have devised, even with the experience of
Massachusetts and New York to aid them.
The Government was in a "wilderness of
woe." Its very existence was threatened.
The booming of hostile cannon could be heard
by the Finance Committee while sitting in the
Treasury Department, consulting with Secretary Chase.

And only those forces that money commanded would silence those threatening guns.
Money in sufficient quantity could not be had

from those who possessed it, unless a rich compensation was offered for its use. Rarely is capital unselfishly patriotic. The organized banks of the country had much of it. Under their control were those securities, whatever they may have been, that were required—or their value—by the Government. And it then became necessary for the Government to use every means to possess them, so far as possible, without actually resorting to forced loans or robbery. Possibly there were two hundred million dollars' worth of State-bank notes in circulation among the people. Those financiers devised a plan to capture most of the values that those notes represented. No matter at what cost to the stockholders of those banks, without regard to the currency of the weak banks, the thing had to be done.

And it was done. The genius of America was equal to the occasion. A great national-bank trust was created. The banking business, or that part of it where currency for circulation among the people was an essential feature, was converted into a monopoly. The monopoly was dealt out among those communities alone that were rich enough in capitalists to lend money to the Government, in consideration of the monopoly offered. The bonds of the Government were exempt from taxation, and for every hundred dollars lent

by such capitalists for such a purpose, the
Government gave its obligation for one hundred dollars, upon which it guaranteed interest in gold, and issued to those capitalists
ninety dollars in paper money, and so legis-
lated that the people were compelled to take
ninety dollars from those capitalists for their
full par value. By forcing the greater number
of the existing banks to close out their other
securities, the Government artificially lessened
the value of all other kinds of securities, in-
cluding municipal and State bonds, and thus
by mere force it appreciated the value of
United States bonds.

It was a stroke of financiering that places
Mr. Chase among the foremost financiers of
the world—if success in getting money for
immediate wants, without regard to future
calamities, be successful financiering.

Hundreds of national banks were organized,
each with its staff equipment of officers. But
in the control of all was a National Comp-
troller with extraordinary powers under the
law—a power purposely given to him—that
practically constituted the system a national-
bank trust. An annual tax of ten per cent. was
put on all other bank notes. From such a trust
the people cannot, now that war necessities
l ave ceased to exist, derive any special benefit, unless it be because of the superiority of

that banking system over all others. When organized, the very monopolistic character of those banks appealed to the selfishness of capital, and, as the Government necessities required that money should be raised at once, to accomplish that purpose the method pursued was possibly the best available one by which to use a bonus.

The evils of monopolies need not be discussed in this book; they are too apparent to the ordinary student of political economy to waste time in their consideration.

If the present national banking system is as perfect as its friends claim it to be, it should within its own resources provide, and consequently control, or rather equitably issue, all the currency notes used by the people of the United States. The coinage of the country, under honest methods, and limited,—as in former years when special legislation was not invoked to create artificial value of the metals used in such coins,—would be limited to the extent of the demands by the people of the United States for those coins, and foreign balances would be adjusted as, in fact, they are now, by the bullion values of the gold coin of the country. Under such conditions there would be but a very limited coinage, and bullion assayed by the Government might more frequently than otherwise be used in the settlement of those balances. But for the Government's indorsement of the purity of the metal used therein, the gold coinage of no country to-day is of any more value to its people than is an equal quantity of gold bullion; and excepting for subsidiary coins, the same is especially true of silver.

Coinage of either gold or silver legal-tender money will probably prove to be more of a menace than a benefit to commerce, until the commercial nations agree upon a ratio of value between the two metals, and upon an agreement to maintain that ratio.

National-bank currency could not be flexible under any conditions other than that of the Government being a creditor to large amounts of the banks; when Congress and the national Treasury Department were incessantly expanding and contracting the Government's indebtedness to those banks as the requirements of the trade of the country for bank bills demanded. The genius has yet to be born that can successfully and satisfactorily execute such an office. Under the present condition it must, of necessity, be steadily contracted as those bonds guaranteeing the national-bank notes fall due. Were the Government to liquidate its indebtedness the national banks would cease to exist,—unless new legislation be resorted to. It could not, under any condition of governmental poverty or wealth, be thoroughly elastic. National banks for deposit purposes, and for such advantages as result from the use of bank checks, cannot, therefore, have any advantage over the private bank or private individual, so long as the private bank or private individual has the confidence of the trading public. They certainly have established no claim to the credit of being able more equitably than other banks to circulate the currency notes among the people. No one has ever given them credit for doing that. But the severest criticism on the national banks has been because of the inequitable distribution of their circulating notes. It was because of that bad feature of the national bank that the Greenback movement was started as early as 1865. And the agitation then begun was sufficient to prevent any of the banks from attempting to tamper with the volume of the currency, as was so successfully attempted with gold coin on that memorable Black Friday. Had there been no Government guarantee of redemption of paper money, Black Friday would have been impossible.

Currency promotes exchange of commodities; lack of currency restricts exchange and causes stagnation in trade. Stagnation in trade causes a reduction in the selling prices of

commodities, and if such stagnation be long
continued, the reduction is to that low point
at which such commodities cannot be dupli-
cated; for labor's reward, in the operation
of duplication, would not sustain life.

This well-known law of trade insures a
profit to the capitalist when withholding currency from tradesmen, although idle money
ceases to be interest-bearing during the
period it is withheld from circulation. When
commodities are forced upon the market at
from twenty-five per cent. to sixty per cent.
below the cost of production, capitalists may
and generally do reap rich rewards. The
shrinkage of values following the contraction
of the currency under Secretary McCullough
was probably far in excess of the amount of
national debt at that time.

Even if the bank officials had exerted all
their forces equitably to distribute their currency notes throughout the country, it was not
in their power to do so, because the natural law
of trade, in times of stringency, tends to the
concentration of the money of a country to
the financially stronger centers, where it really
is least needed. And thus the drain is from
the financially weaker centers, where it is
most needed. There is absolutely no flexi-
bility in the national-bank currency, and to
meet an extraordinary demand it could not be

expanded. In this respect the national banking system is defective. And that fault has been most keenly felt throughout the country during the last thirty years. This, too, is a fault so grievous that it constitutes the present national banking system—not "a great blessing," but a real calamity.

The objection to free banking, or to a restriction of a monopoly of the national bank, or to the Government abandoning the banking business, seems to rest largely upon the theory that the money issued by free banks will prove inconvenient money to travel with.

The fact is, the great majority of the American people do not travel far enough from their own home to carry a good bank bill beyond the range of its face value. Only the foolish or dishonest would attempt to travel by using worthless bank bills. If they lived in the immediate vicinity of a bank and the bills of that bank were not at par, it would be because the managers of that bank had not inspired the people living within its vicinity—who knew them well—with implicit confidence. Such banks could not circulate their bills; the people, distrusting those who managed the bank, would not accept them.

If the State bank or the free bank would stimulate healthy business in its immediate neighborhood, the amount of the benefit de-

rived from that stimulation would unquestionably be infinitely more profitable than would
be the loss from the inconvenience arising
from the State-bank notes not being as convenient a currency with which to travel.

It is not necessary to enter into any argument to prove the necessity for the use of
paper money. To an extent yet unheard of
business could be conducted or managed without a single coin, or without a currency based
upon the value of coin. Coin values fluctuate, and the cause of that fluctuation is the
supply and demand of the precious metal. A
Secretary of the Treasury of the United States,
shortly after the discovery of the immense
gold fields in California, in a serious public
paper addressed to the President of the
United States, expressed alarm because of a
calamity likely to fall upon the country,—
from the cheap gold of the new mines driving
silver out of the country. Less than a quarter
of a century later, another Secretary of the
Treasury addressed a similar communication
to the President, in which he deplores the
calamity likely to fall upon the country from
cheap silver depleting the country of its gold.
The fact is, neither gold nor silver is essential
to the successful conducting of the business
of the country. That is a fallacy that has
twice within this century nearly wrecked the

Bank of England. And each time the disaster was averted by the use of paper money.

Business is conducted now, not by man's faith in the value of a coin, but by man's faith in his fellow-man. A business man of to-day trusts his fellow-man, not because that man has gold, but because he has business and personal integrity. Man's faith in his fellow-man is to-day the foundation upon which business rests; and checks, bank notes, and promises to pay are essentially necessary only to make the wheels of business run smoothly.

The bank located in the country districts does not, under the present system, afford to the farmer or country operator any accommodation whatever except when money is cheap. In straitened financial times, when the farmer or country manufacturer, as well as the merchant, needs financially bridging over, he can get but very little assistance from the bank; and the reason of it is clear. The circulating medium is gathered to the money centers as soon as any stringency in the money market becomes apparent; and however firm may be the bank officers' faith in the business tact and the personal integrity of the country farmer or the country merchant, it is not within their power to lend him money; the demand from the money centers having exhausted the supply of bank bills to the lowest point that it is possible for the bank to reach and yet live.

The argument that the notes of State banks would be more likely to be kept at home than either the Government fiat notes or the national-bank bills, many financiers dismiss with a sneer. Mr. Blaine said, "We would keep it—State-bank money—at home, because it would be so worthless nobody would take it abroad." No one of good judgment would take State-bank bills abroad to pay traveling expenses with, because only very few with whom one would have to transact business would have sufficient confidence in the genuine character of the bill, or confidence enough in its maker, to accept it in payment, especially as payment could be exacted in a currency with which they were perfectly conversant. This objection to State-bank notes applies with equal force to national-bank bills, and to Bank of England notes, excepting that those notes have a wider range of acquaintances. Yet at the proper distance from or nearness to the place of issuance, any of those bills are readily exchangeable for currency that will be acceptable in that quarter of the world to which the traveler may wish to go. If a traveler be not sufficiently intelligent to effect such an ex-

change before he sets out upon his jour-
ney, he would, under any provision of
Government for his protection, most probably
be put to much loss and great inconvenience
before he got very far on his way in the distant country through which he was to travel.
Had he a pocketful of gold disks, each of
the value of ten dollars, their purity attested
by a stamp of the bankers Rothschilds, not one
out of each hundred men and women he met
in a business way would, on the security of
one of those gold disks, trust him out of their
sight with fifty cents' worth of commodities,
There are, doubtless, many counties in this
American Union where not a business man
has any knowledge of the appearance of a
Bank of England note; and not a hotel keeper
in many of the counties would trust a traveler
with a night's lodging on the security of a ten-
pound note of that bank, unless there was
something about the traveler himself that impressed the hotel keeper with faith in his integrity. Over all this land there are thousands
of places where men are trusted upon the
lines in their faces alone, whereas a bagful of
notes of the Bank of France would not promote the credit of a dollar.

A circulating currency for the benefit of
travelers is not what is wanted, but a currency
for the benefit of people who stay at home,

who form business communities, who transact the business, and develop the possibilities of such communities. And a currency that is most convenient for travelers is, in times of financial distress, almost certain to be least beneficial to small, undeveloped communities. It is that feature of the State bank,—that its currency will stay at home,—which many deem worthy of a sneer only,—that is alone of any real value in any bank, excepting the benefit derived from a bank of deposit, and from the convenience of the check system offered to the business public by such banks.

The simple fiat money of the Government may be the most convenient money for people traveling through the country that issues it. There is no logical objection to a limited quantity of such currency issued on a basis of taxation, and made legal tender for taxes, but not for private debts.

National-bank bills have no advantage over the bills of a State bank, excepting that given them by the guarantee of the Government— that their face values will be paid in legal-tender money. It is nothing more nor less than fiat money. No responsibility rests upon any individual should those notes not be paid in coin values, adjusted by the commercial world on the basis of bullion values of the precious metals. There is no provision for the redemption of those bills in gold if the struggle of free-silver coiners were to result in the triumph of the silver party. Should that happen, the value of the American gold dollar will possibly be appreciated fully sixty per cent. Under the discount of a fraction of one per cent. it would soon be withdrawn from circulation, and the American legal-tender note, based on silver bullion, would then be discounted in Europe at a rate regulated wholly by the value of bullion silver.

That the currency bills of State and private banks are more likely to remain in circulation near their point of issue than Government notes or national-bank bills, is a well-attested fact. And that fact makes these private and State-bank notes vastly superior to the Government bill. For, it was the very purpose for which that bill was passed that those private and State banks or a bank of the national-bank system were constituted. This primarily was for the convenience of the people living near such banks, and to develop more thoroughly the possibilities of the communities in which they were located.

It has been shown that, under the national-bank system, currency bills—money—at times were attracted away from those localities where the greatest real necessity for their presence existed, to localities of more financial force but of less necessity; and always at a great inconvenience and cost to the people living in these financially weaker localities. Such would not be the case with State-bank bills. This an apt illustration will plainly show.

A State bank of Delaware, under a system of banking so radically liberal as to appall many conservative bankers of the hour, was chartered with the privilege of issuing three dollars in currency bills for each dollar in coin, legal-tender currency of the United States, that was held by the bank in its vaults. Of course there were conditions imposed on the officers of the bank to secure safety of the bank-note holders, but so far only as police-regulation laws for collection of debts can secure. Those bills could be issued only on ample security that they would, when returned to the bank in the course of trade, be redeemed at their full face value. Such bills could lawfully be paid out only to depositors in the place of money they had already deposited in the bank, or on notes indorsed by acceptable indorsers, or for other reasonable securities. The loans made on notes were made by bank officers who were personally acquainted with the maker of the note, whose business and private habits were thoroughly known to them. Consequently, " honesty,

sobriety, economy, and good business habits "
were, when taken collectively, really bankable
values, and, substantially, were capital.

Men possessing such capital should be encouraged to exert their talent and wealth to
develop the possibilities of the communities
in which they live.

And that is what that bank and other like
banks in Delaware did, before they were
throttled by the bank-note tax of 1866. It
was not State pride nor patriotism that
prompted the managers of those banks to
encourage—by lending their bills—those
sober, honest, economical, and capable business men to develop the possibilities of their
communities. Patriotism, more frequently
than otherwise, when reduced to the basis of
dollars and cents, is a low-priced article. It
was from the interest-money that the bank
managers could gather from lending their currency that they derived their profits. And as
the currency bills would not be accepted at
face value very far from the banking house,
it was necessary for the bank managers to encourage business men within the limits of
their acquaintance and locality to develop
those industries that would demand the use
of the currency bills. It was of little advantage for such banks to lend their bills to someone living in a remote community. Had the

officers of the Bank of Dover, in illustration, lent five thousand dollars face value of their bills to a man engaged in developing an enterprise in Lancaster County, Pennsylvania, that man would in all probability have deposited those bills in a Lancaster County bank, and, although the Lancaster County bank president may have been an intimate friend of the president of the Bank of Dover,—with the uttermost confidence in his integrity—those Dover Bank bills would have been sent with the speediest dispatch back to that bank.

Such is the force of the law of trade. The bills of the Bank of Dover were only certificates of credit. Only by lending its credit could the Bank of Dover make a profit on the loan made to the Lancaster County man. If the certificates of credit were returned to the bank, and legal-tender money demanded for them within three days, it follows that the Bank of Dover lent its credit for three days, and could realize therefrom only the interest on a three days' loan, in which transaction of course there would be no profit. The Bank of Dover could not have been profitably conducted if the business of the bank had not been confined to the immediate vicinity of Dover, where bills of that bank furnished the currency of the community, and where the greater part of the bills—money—deposited

by the business men as security for the payment of the checks or drafts drawn on that
bank by its depositors, were notes of the Bank
of Dover, and, as profit-making bills while in
its vaults, were as valuable to that bank as if
in the pockets of the various members of the
community of Dover. To lend its credit to
persons engaged in developing the business
possibilities of the vicinity of Dover, was absolutely necessary for the existence of that bank,
and consequently the most active motive of its
officers was to induce persons to encourage
the business activity in the vicinity of Dover.

Under the banking system of to-day, beyond the encouragement that interest-making
may prompt bank managers to extend ac-
commodations to their depositors, there is no
motive to prompt managers of banks to dis-
criminate between lending money to the business men of their own centers and to a man in
a center hundreds of miles away.

It is urged, as an objection to any form of
free banking, that there is too great an inducement to an overissue of bank bills. Ful-
lerton, in his " Regulation of Currency," p.
83, says: " It may be stated, therefore, as a
settled principle, that the efforts of banks of
issue to extend their circulation know no re-
mission; that the whole system, in fact, is
continually on the stretch, and that but for

the antagonistic force which is always in
action to correct and repress it, the overflow
of notes would be irresistible. Upon this
ground alone, then, there seems to me to be
an effectual negative to the supposition that
the fluctuation of the bank-note circulation
depends on the discretion of the bankers. A
man who always puts forth his whole strength
has no further effort left to make."

Bankers who purpose to make a profit from
the sale of their financial credit cannot afford
to impair that credit, and from that " force "
—antagonistic to an overissue of bills—they
will not lend their credit—their bills—to those
they believe will not return it or proper substitutes in payment of the discounted notes on
which the loan was made. They will not willingly make unsafe loans, because they cannot
conduct their bank successfully if they do.
There can be no stronger reason given why
an overissue of currency bills is nearly
impossible. Should the bank officers attempt an overissue, by lending money to
reckless men, it would at once impair
the credit of the bank to such an extent
that depositors would decline to do business
with it, and reputable business men who borrow from banks on the semi-official assurance
of its managers—that at the time of payment
their paper will be extended if conditions be

favorable—would not trust their enterprise on the promise of such men. Consequently, such a bank could not keep its notes in circulation or do a banking business. A banker cannot sell his credit to a community that has no faith in the integrity or good judgment of the banker; because that credit is of no value. Bills issued by such a banker would not pass current in the community—consequently could not be put into circulation. Even such good paper currency as that of Canada cannot be circulated in the United States. Therefore the assumption that irresponsible bankers can circulate their notes is an absurdity.

While the active motive that controls the banker is to issue as many bills as possible, he is, nevertheless, restrained by well-established business principles of value for value from overissuing them. Hence there would be issued, even under such a "wild-cat" banking system as that of the illustrative Bank of Dover, only the amount of currency demanded by the safe business interests of the community in whose interest the bank had been organized. No more, no less. And the expansion and contraction of the circulating currency in such a community would be governed entirely by the safe business requirements of that community.

The local bank, whether a State or a private

bank, the payment of whose notes is not guaranteed by the Government of a great central
bank is, for reasons already shown, the most
desirable bank to promote business possibilities in the locality in which it is situated.
And, further, as it works no unjust disadvantage to any other bank located within its own
or any other locality, it is therefore the best
possible form of banking for that locality.
Collectively, such banks are the best adapted,
justly and vigorously, to develop the business
possibilities of the entire country.

CHAPTER VII.

In dealing with the currency question it is proper, it is imperative, that the question should be considered from the view-point of justice. If justice demand the demonitization of silver, with its subsequent appreciation of the purchasing power of gold, then, only lasting good can come to the country from placing our currency on the basis of gold. If, on the other hand, the unlimited coinage of silver, with its consequent debasement of purchasing power of our unit be just, the nation should at once resort to free coinage, and coin into money all the silver that would be offered to it for that purpose, and in the coinage use such energy that all the silver offered for coinage should be converted into coin at the speediest possible rate.

There can be no doubt that to make those silver dollars fast enough, such unlimited coinage of silver, which permitted a holder of one thousand dollars' worth of silver bullion to pay two thousand dollars of debts, would make great demands upon the facilities of the mints. There is but little doubt that silver bullion would advance in price; for a time, at least. If, therefore, the purchasing power of silver bullion should, under such influence, steadily increase until sixteen ounces of it would purchase the same quantity of commodities that one ounce of gold would, the purchasing power of gold not having been disturbed in the meantime, no permanent enhancement of other values would, of course, take place, and, consequently, only the few who pay their debts, and the bullion holders, and the silver miners would be benefited by the free coinage of silver. If the purchasing power of gold would be depreciated under the influence of free-silver coinage, and the values of other commodities be appreciated, as would probably be the case, all possessors of commodities would reap a benefit that probably might greatly stimulate business.

There are two distinct classes in every civilized land, and doubtless such classes will exist as long as civilization lasts; they are the debtor and the creditor. The misfortunes of the debtor class offer no logical reason why superior advantage should be granted to them; nor do the wealth and the influence that wealth gives offer any reason why such advantage should be given to the creditor class, although they may be, as many of their friends assert they are, God's natural leaders of the people. If to frame laws to provide currency for the people it is necessary that special privileges should be extended to the one or the other of these two classes, it is proper, then, that we determine which of these two classes best serve the interest of the country. If, in the consideration of this matter, we would be governed by the words of the Divine Master, there is then no question that we should legislate so that the burden would fall lightly, if at all, upon the debtor class. Philanthropy, Christianity, and selfish brutality, on the other hand, all unite in declaring that if either the debtor or the creditor class must suffer by currency legislation, the burden should fall entirely upon the creditor class.

However, before arriving at a conclusion, it is well first to consider which of the two classes are of the greatest benefit to the entire people; which of these two classes add to the country's ornamentation, to the glories that clothe our person in comfort and fill our soul with pride. Is it the debtor or the creditor class? Is it the user or the lender of money?

Of the people endowed by their Creator with a modicum of common sense but few assert that such credit belongs principally to the creditor class. This, of course, is not intended as a reflection on that class. For the man who has reached that point in life at which he can begin to lend money, and thus become a creditor, is to be respected, if, of course, he have reached that point by industrious and honorable methods. Nor is he to be despised because some energetic ancestor provided him with the privilege of being a creditor all the days of his life. But to ascribe superior usefulness to such persons is simply adulation, absurdity, or imbecility.

The creditor seeks to lend money, and the energy used in seeking such investments is, more frequently than otherwise, a hired agent of the creditor. Consequently, a creditor does not seek to lend his money in order that some enterprise, needed to develop the country, should be promoted, but rather that to the creditor there should be a handsome return for the money advanced. It is true that there are a few men in the land possessed of capital who would prefer lending money in their own country to lending it to people living in other countries for higher rates of interest when absolutely certain that the investment in either country would be safe. The generous public denominates such men cranks. Not one-hundredth part of one per cent. of the capital of the country held by the creditor class would be lent for business operations in the country if it were given an investment as absolutely safe, and as convenient, outside the country at a higher rate of interest. Therefore, to claim that the creditor class is entitled to special benefits, because it is the leader selected to direct the business of the country in such channels as are calculated to make it prosperous, is simply absurd.

For the same selfish reasons, perhaps, the man of the debtor class who borrows money does so that he may grow richer and have more comforts. But to do so it is then necessary for him to put forth an hitherto undeveloped energy; an energy that can be developed only by the help of additional capital. He does not, it is true, seek to build up a great factory and extend his operations over the States and Territories for the sole purpose of advancing the prosperity of the country, but he does advance it, nevertheless, and he has no opportunity to shift his field of operation, as the creditor has. He stands very much in the same position that the boy did who was digging out the woodchuck—had to get that´ woodchuck; because, " no woodchuck, no dinner." So it is, therefore, from the energy and intelligence of the debtor class that the material prosperity of the land must come.

Nor is the creditor class essential to the material prosperity of the land. The great West was built up and made rich and fertile without any assistance from the creditor. And after it had become rich, after its miles upon miles of prairie lands were made fertile, under the manipulation of earnest energy, after towns and cities had covered it, capital was directed thither largely from the East; and the Western people to-day assert that the introduction of money-lenders among them was the beginning of the ruin and disaster that have laid the West in the position it now occupies —of almost enslavement to Eastern capital.

If, in legislating, we should be governed by the principle of "the greatest good to the greatest number," we would be induced to lend the greatest assistance to the debtor class. To just what extent the debtor class outnumbers the creditor class, or that part of it that sells or rents to others the use of money, it is difficult to ascertain. But that it does outnumber them— and very largely so—is a fact no one can gainsay. Therefore, " good politics " would direct that legislation on the subject of currency should be toward lessening the burdens of the debtor class. It is not easy to determine who are the debtors and who are the creditors; for in every avenue of trade the products of the operator become his debtor, and he is the creditor of his products.

The builder of machinery who spends days and weeks in developing a machine finds, when he finishes it, that all the energy he has expended is represented in the machine that he has produced. That machine is his debtor, he is the creditor. If legislation is so shaped—assuming that legislation can affect the value of that machine—that the result of this man's labor is enhanced in value, he reaps a greater reward as creditor; but if, to the contrary, legislation is so manipulated that the value of the machine is depreciated, he becomes so much the poorer. This illustration is used to demonstrate the fact that, if even but one individual be working as his own master to produce commodities that other men require, he may be seriously affected by pernicious laws.

The farmer who spends a year's labor, or at least waits a year to produce his crop, also finds himself either reaping the reward or suffering the calamities that arise from favorable or unfavorable legislation. He purchases his fertilizers in the month of August, at a price that is made by a given standard. He lends it to the land, to be repaid for it by the crop harvested in the following July. If the standard of value, by any cause whatsoever, be changed within that year, the farmer receives his pay from the harvest at a different rate, unless that which he produces should have its value appreciated exactly in the line with the change in the value of the measure—money.

However, if that farmer should contract to pay for the fertilizers to be used on his ground with the proceeds of the sales of the harvest, and the standard of value should, in the meantime, be changed in a direction that made it more difficult for him to obtain the money, or, in other words, that compelled him to sell more of the products of his farm and labor to procure it than at the time of the purchase, it follows, then, that the farmer has an additional burden imposed upon him,—a result of such changes in the money measure that he was not called upon to contemplate at the time he made his contract, and which strict justice does not demand that he should pay.

If the manufacturer of the fertilizers should, by the very reverse of this change in the value of money, be compelled to receive less than the existing conditions then made just, an injustice would be done to the manufacturer of the fertilizers.

There is another large class of business men that it would be very difficult to class either with the debtors or the creditors. They are those dealers in merchandise who possess stocks of goods, who owe money for goods purchased, who have money owing to them for goods sold. It is fair to assume that, aside from the inconvenience that arises —we may say momentarily—in settling balances among the class of men above described, no serious inconvenience could be felt by them either by the appreciation or the depreciation of the purchasing power of the gold dollar.

From the appreciation of the value of the dollar, the wage-earner derives an advantage for such a length of time only as may be required to adjust wages to the old unfortunate standard, namely, just as small a sum as wage-payers can induce wage-earners to work for, which sum is usually measured by the minimum of man's wants.

Any depreciation of the value of the American dollar would work to the disadvantage of the American wage-earner, thereby materially lessening his ability to procure those things that go to make life comfortable. The enforced idler can derive little, if any, advantage from it—none, when his money gives out. If the old wages should be maintained when that dollar had depreciated to its lowest limit, then wage-earners would be reduced to a greater degree of privation than that they now are compelled to endure. If the depreciation of the dollar be carried to an extent beyond his ability to purchase those comforts of life that would but satisfy his wants, he would then simply begin an aggressive movement for increased wages, and would resort to those measures that in the past have been successful in attaining such objects. And from the time of the beginning of the depreciation of the purchasing power of the dollar, to the time that resulted in an adjustment of the wages, and back again from that period until he had succeeded in placing himself on the same plane of the purchasing power of wages that he stands on to-day, he would be the loser by the depreciation of the purchasing power of our dollar.

A uniform fall in prices is not the result of overproduction of commodities,—if such an economic condition be possible,—but of an appreciation of the value of the standard measure. Trading with the assistance of money is but improved bartering.

If, for example, certain men had horses that they valued at one hundred units, and other men possessed oxen that they valued at the same number of units, and these valuations were mutual, what difference would it make to these men if,

when they desired to exchange horses
for oxen, those horses and oxen were valued
a year previously at one hundred and fifty
units? And if all the other commodities useful to man had from the preceding year depreciated to a greater or less extent than horses
and oxen, men would perforce use more of
those commodities than in the preceding year.
There would be no overproduction. But if
there had been an increased demand for one
of those commodities—gold—useful to man,
and that commodity had been selected as the
standard, the demand then for debt-paying
and interest requirement would compel many
people to sell their oxen and horses so as to
procure gold to meet those requirements.
Men could not exchange oxen for horses;
they would each probably be compelled to exchange the greater part of their oxen and
horses for gold, to obtain money with which
to pay their indebtedness; an indebtedness
contracted when those oxen were worth one
hundred and fifty units.

Falling prices, measured by labor's compensation, invariably cause much hardship to
those of our citizens who have borrowed
money for industrial improvements. On the
other hand, they certainly add to the reward
of those who live upon the energy of others.
Every man, woman, and child, and their pet

animals live upon the energy of others who derive their income from bonds, mortgages, and rents. Nor are those the only ones living upon the energy of others. The fact that men, by energy and sagacity, may reach a condition in this life by which they may live comfortably and honored upon the energy of others is perhaps the most active, the most useful force at work to make them progressive.

The creditor class, which largely controls the use of money, is composed of those people who own bank stock and railroad stock, who hold mortgages against other property, and own real estate, and owe practically no debts. While this class is not numerically very large, it has for the last thirty years largely influenced the legislation of our country. It is unquestionably true that nearly all men who belong to this class are in favor of any currency that will make it more difficult for the debtor class to pay interest on any debts other than those guaranteed by safe security. There is a consensus of opinion among them, doubtless, that the demonetizing of silver and the adopting of gold as the single standard of measure would best serve their ends.

A large percentage of debtors is composed of those who have secured loans upon real property, that they assume they will not be

compelled to pay for so long as they pay the
interest demanded for the loan, and maintain
the property offered as security in the same
valuable condition as it was at the time
the loan was effected. This represents the
enterprising, struggling man; this represents those who have purchased lots upon
which they have built homes, expecting to
pay off their mortgages a little at a time until,
from their savings, they may be enabled to
liquidate the entire indebtedness and become
sole owner of the property. In this class are
many small dealers, struggling professional
men, and wage-earners. Another portion, and
a very large portion, of this class may be
found in the agricultural districts, where
young, enterprising men have purchased
tracts of land more or less improved, paying
only a part of the purchase money, and placing
a mortgage on the property for the remainder.
When these mortgages are made on such
given property by young men, they, more frequently than otherwise, calculate, when making that purchase, that it will be the struggle
of their life to release themselves from this
indebtedness. In other words, the mortgaged farm stands to them in the same relation that the savings bank stands to the wage-
earners; it is the means by which they can
gradually save their earnings.

Hence, it requires but very little effort of the human mind to reach the conclusion that the class of men here defined as the debtor class is the class from which we must hope that the material prosperity of our country shall be advanced; specially when we add to it another portion of the debtor class—the manufacturers—which erects large plants for producing those commodities that society demands for its comforts. These factories are almost universally erected by men who invest less than one-half the cost of them; who go into debt for the other part. Were they possessed of the idea that the money they borrow for the beginning of such industries would be demanded in a few months, or even a few years, many of those enterprises would never be begun. Therefore, it is a fair assumption to say that the material progress of our country depends upon the energy displayed in the future, as in the past, by men who voluntarily enter the debtor class.

If currency legislation must be so shaped that to one or the other of these classes special privileges are extended, then common reason demands that the privilege should be extended to the debtor class.

CHAPTER VIII.

THE value of money, like that of any other commodity, is affected by the law of supply and demand. Those whose wealth is all in money have an advantage over those whose wealth is in another commodity. The owners of money may readily effect an exchange for any one or more of the thousands of kinds of commodities that constitute the wealth of the world; while the owners of those other commodities can exchange theirs for money only, unless—which so frequently happens—they can satisfactorily barter with their neighbors, or resort to warehouse-exchange system, by giving to a middleman a part of their commodities, to effect for them acceptable exchanges. The latter system is practically that of the country stores already described. Under it, communities may prosper, people be healthfully fed, comfortably housed and clothed, made happy and fairly contented. There can, however, be no marked progress in such communities, a disadvantage, perhaps, compensated for by the general exemption from poverty; for usually there is in unprogressive communities no abject poverty unless there is retrogression, or as a consequence of dissolute living.   But this latter is not commonly indulged in where such communities exist.

Money, although it is a commodity, possesses a privilege or a purchasing power other commodities do not possess.   It is this privilege money possesses that should be restricted within its legitimate sphere.   If a certain number of money-owners—necessarily but few —control the supply of money so as to artificially take from other commodities a part of their value, which the law of supply and demand for those commodities would not have reduced, it follows, then, that business principles, truth, and justice alike, demand that such power of money should be limited to a minimum if, by the condition of things, it be impossible to restrict it entirely.   Money cannot be made to affect the values of other commodities so long as it remains an unchanged measure; but, unlike the yardstick, the unit of money is not an inflexible standard.

Gold, to-day, is the money measure of the world; it matters not which metal may be the standard of a nation.   Gold measures the value of other commodities, not as the index figures on the thermometer indicate the degree of heat, but rather as the mercury measures the temperature. The figures of the thermometer are inflexible. But the mercury in the glass tube is not more flexible in indicating the temperature than is gold in measuring commodity values. So energetic, in fact, is the fluctuation of the value of gold that, probably, were it possible to gauge it, not a minute of time would fail to disclose a change. Yet, doubtless, it is as staple in its value in relation to the mean values of all other commodities as any other single commodity could ever be expected to be, and if a single commodity be most desirable as a basis for money, gold, doubtless, is the very best that could be selected. The advantage of using more than one metal as a basis for money, if there be such advantage, lies in the fact that there is less likelihood to be any violent changes in the value of each of the metals at the same time; and, again, that the money-dealers cannot so readily command the world's production of two commodities as they can of one. It may be forcibly urged that, if to the world's debtors there be given always the option of the two metals they may use for the paying of their debts, they will invariably use the cheaper; and that at times, when extraordinary productions of the one and not a lessening of the productions of the other cause a cheapening of the value of that metal, the debtors would not be obliged to make full payment for values received. Indeed, if an option of paying their debts with the cheapest of these metals had been given to the debtors by the laws of the world during the past two hundred years, the basis, then, of the world's money to-day would be copper; if for two thousand years, it would be iron.

Iron, copper, brass, wood, woven fabrics are all used as substitutes for the standard yardstick. In our country it is also the right of every purchaser of commodities that are sold by the yard, to demand that the yardstick used in measuring shall be of exactly the same dimensions—or value as a measure —as the standard yardstick kept by the Government, which is securely guarded at Washington. That yardstick is never used except to measure the accuracy of other yardsticks. The yardsticks in use are made of almost every conceivable material, and are all substitutes for the yardstick. Even those that have been officially stamped as yardsticks, may be questioned as accurate standard measures; but doubtless ninety-nine per cent. of the volume of business transacted in the United States where yardsticks are needed, is done by the use of unstamped and unguaranteed yardsticks. On the other hand, the proportion of short measurement—because of wantonly-debased yardsticks—is so small that figures will scarcely express the minuteness of the percentage.

It is just as easy to use a substitute for money as for the yardstick. In fact, the merchants of the present time would scarcely be able to transact business without a substitute for money. So any measure that seeks to prevent a man from substituting anything that will more expeditiously enable him by the use of money to effect exchanges of commodities, when such substitutions deprive no other man of a just right, is a measure of oppression, and should not, therefore, find a place in the economic system of any, much less of a free, people.

Upward of two hundred years ago Sir Thomas Gresham, after a careful study of the logic of the question and of the facts presented to him as a merchant in money, formulated the law that bears his name. No man of to-day who gives serious thought to the subject can reason himself into the belief of a possibility of Gresham's proposition not being correct. Upward of two thousand years before Gresham was born there was a civilization on earth that few will dispute was even more advanced in civilization—save in the science of war and destruction—than was England in Gresham's time.

Among the great masters of thought of that day was one of whom England has yet failed to produce his superior, or even his equal— the great Plato. It is said of Plato, that after years of thoughtful observation of the use of money and its various substitutes in Athens, he formulated a law that, although well-nigh forgotten, may be of even more importance to the economic world than was Gresham's law. In effect, Plato's law declared that " the money best calculated to develop the material welfare of communities was a money that, in such communities, could readily be ex- changed at its face value for the best money of the world, but of so little value intrinsically that it would not be attracted away from the community in which it was issued." It was for the convenience of the Athenians that Plato advocated the use of a money that would possess all the value in Athens that the best money could possess, but could not be made as valuable in Athens or elsewhere when melted in the pot.

There are many substitutes for money. That which now serves best as a substitute is the check, and as a means of effecting changes of credit in the system of bookkeeping to which banks of deposit have perfected it, it is invaluable. The extent to which it may be advantageously used is possibly scarcely yet conjectured. In China, where the population is dense and transportation is slow, it is almost the only means of paying debts, and checks are used there in paying the very smallest accounts. Europe is much indebted to Asia for its intellectual development; and, doubtless, Europe may still learn from Asia much more that will be useful. In the arts and science of war and destruction of man's creations, the Europeans are masters. But are they in the science of peace? Money of gold and silver is the money of war. Paper money and bank checks are the substitute for money, which peace promotes and war destroys. And why? The value of gold and silver money rests upon the value of the metal used. Wars do not disturb it. The value of paper money rests entirely on the public's confidence in the ability of its makers to pay on demand the amount named on the face of the paper. War impairs that confidence.

Paper issued as money by a government that guarantees its redemption in coin, cannot be classed as a substitute for money, but rather as money itself. Paper issued and serving in the place of money not made legal tender by State or nation is a substitute for money. Paper used as money that may be issued by State or nation, and receivable for taxes, would also be a substitute for money.

There can be no doubt that paper bills that are not legal tenders may successfully and advantageously be used in business, which no creditor is under obligation to take. But no such paper will be accepted by a creditor who does not feel confident that such paper will be redeemed by its maker for its full face-value on demand. There can be no doubt that so far as the business affairs of the United States are concerned, paper money, not legal tenders, has frequently been most advantageously used; notably, the generous use of Clearing House certificates in 1893. There is no reason for believing that its use has been less advantageous to the other commercial nations of the world.

In small communities substitutes for money have an advantage over money itself that makes them an invaluable aid in the building up of agrarian interests. Thus, communities that produce large supplies of those commodities that society needs, should not be impoverished by such great production. Nothing but unnatural causes will produce the condition of poverty now existing in such communities. Under the present monetary system of civilization it frequently happens that many die of hunger, surrounded by an " overproduction " of food. They die also for the want of clothing, surrounded by an " overproduction " of clothing. They sicken and suffer, too, in the stifling atmosphere of the accursed tenement-houses, surrounded by an " overproduction " of houses. In the agrarian districts, however, few suffer for the want of plenty of air. They do suffer, though, for want of wholesome food and want of comfortable clothing. And that, too, in communities where they have performed their full share of labor in producing an abundance of those commodities that could usually be produced advantageously in the community in which they live.

No man will attempt to justify the system that causes men to suffer for food and clothing who have faithfully and successfully labored to produce those commodities they had every reason to suppose would command for them those things necessary for comfort.

No man will fail to condemn a system that he believes will be instrumental in preventing men from enjoying the fruit of their labor, unless he have a selfish motive for such prevention.

When the Government of the United States enforces its declaration that no money, or substitute for money, not equal in value to the best money issued by the Government, which is a gold dollar, shall be used in the States, it then places an impediment in the way of the people of Illustrateville to enjoy the fruits of their labor.

CHAPTER IX.

ILLUSTRATEVILLE is a town, let us say, of about three thousand inhabitants, surrounded by fertile farms. It was settled upward of a hundred years ago by a class of worthy, frugal, industrious young farmers. At least, those settlers possessed themselves of the lands comprised within the community of which Illustrateville is the center. The town itself was a result of this settlement. To-day two or more competing railroads pass through it, offering to its citizens as favorable opportunities—such as cheap passenger and freight rates—as are possessed by any other town of its size in the country.

The growth of the town was slow; no artificial boom developed it unnaturally. A half dozen or more young farmers a hundred years ago—each with his wife and small family, and a family outfit, more or less elaborate—had traveled overland from the place of their birth until they had reached this place. Each man had, as his great ambition, the desire to till his own farm, to rear his children to honesty of purpose, justly to perform the duties of life, to be respected by his neighbors, and to provide a comfortable sustenance for his family against the time when old age would deprive him of physical power to produce further.

The land was fertile, the climate agreeable, and many things about the country were so pleasing that these early settlers sent to those they left behind such information about the settlement that others were induced to come.

Soon the need of a school was felt; a convenient spot was selected by a committee appointed for the purpose; and everyone united to do his portion toward the erecting of the schoolhouse. It stood completed, the first house built in Illustrateville. One of the farmers, whose house was near the school, decided that the demand of the new community required a store. This he opened, together, possibly, with a public house. The schoolhouse had served as a place of public worship, but the demands of the advanced prosperity of the settlement required a church and a resident pastor. The agriculturists' requirements for a blacksmith had induced a smith to set up his forge near the church, and in a little while a wheelwright shop was connected with the blacksmith shop, and a resident wheelwright was added to the community. A post office had already been established by the

Government, and a stage-route to a larger supply town became a necessity. An energetic and restless printer had entered the community and set up a printing office, which was but the prelude to a newspaper. A resident physician had long before been added to the community. Following the issuing of a newspaper came also the lawyer.

It had, as may be surmised, taken a decade or more before the town had reached this state of development.

Later, then, some of the more thrifty or more fortunate of the farmers had concluded that they would give up their farm to a son, and move into the town, there to spend their remaining years in retirement from active labor. Each of this class built for himself in the town a more or less pretentious house; and so the town grew, until, after many years, six or seven hundred houses had been erected in Illustrateville. In many of these houses, and, in fact, in most of them, dwelt young, active persons, children or dependents of the household, who longed for the opportunity to earn a livelihood. Illustrateville had indeed many charms for them, and the mere thought of leaving it and going out among strangers was generally oppressive. At home nearly everybody knew them. It was known that they had been reared in eminently respectable homes; known, too, who their grandparents were, as well as their parents. Everybody, in fact, knew the eminent respectability of their lineage. Sufficiently informed by education to know the consideration that they received in Illustrateville was because of their respectable lineage, the same would not, they knew, be accorded them elsewhere, and that if they were of what is termed " the humble class " their lines of life, if sustenance could there be obtained, would run smoother in Illustrateville than elsewhere on earth.

So long as the sole industry was simply purveying to the needs of the agriculturists who surrounded the town, it was necessary for a majority of these young people to go away to the larger towns and to the cities. To prevent this exodus of the very best material for commercial developments that the town possessed, measures were sought to establish industries in the town for the production of those commodities other than their own community would consume. Illustrateville and its vicinity possessed the material, the skill, and the labor essential to the manufacturing of several important and much-used commodities, which could readily be sold for use in other communities. The town had the reputation of being a rich community; and, in truth, it was rich. Nearly every man lived in his own house, around which was more or less fertile and highly cultivated land. The houses were well supplied with comfortable furniture; a large number of the householders were owners of one or more horses, and nearly all had a sum of money saved by—hidden away in some secure place. Want and privation were truly strangers in Illustrateville; although not one of its inhabitants would have been called a capitalist by those who fully understood what that term implies.

At a meeting of the business men and property-holders, called to discuss plans for promoting new industries in Illustrateville, it became apparent that the wish that such manufacturing industries should be established as would keep the young and energetic men and women at home, was practically unanimous. Discussion of the question of the ways and means of accomplishing that object revealed that there was not sufficient cash capital in the town to be of much service toward securing the object sought after; yet there was an abundance of wealth. There were very few mortgaged houses in the community, but those few served to measure the available worth of the town. It was found that fifteen or twenty of the community's citizens could readily borrow, on the security of

their farms and buildings, upward of one
hundred thousand dollars.

Under existing conditions, had those fifteen
or twenty men determined to establish given
industries necessary to keep the young energy
of the town at home, it would have been
necessary for them to organize a company.
To secure the cash capital necessary for its
establishing, they would have had to go to
some distant and more general business center, and there, on the security of mortgages on
their individual holding, borrow the necessary
money. The men who would organize such
a business, and by such methods, would not
be old men of conservative habits, who, satisfied with their accumulation, were perfectly
willing to live in a simple way and aid younger
men; they would, on the contrary, be the
speculative men of the community, who would
intend actively to manage the business that
they organized. Whether they organized
that business from the purest philanthropy or
from the basest selfish motives, the conditions
confronting them would be the same. Under
existing conditions they could not have borrowed the money except at a time when there
was a redundancy of money in the great business centers; for, under no other conditions
of the money market could such loans be
effected on country property.

It may be well to examine what has been the result in the United States during the last thirty-five years, of nearly all manufacturing industries, that have been established by the efforts of the more prosperous and enterprising members of communities such as Illustrateville, to promote home industries. In times of sluggish business conditions throughout the country but few such industries were ever established; in times of panics and business depression, none it is safe to say has ever been organized. Only at such times as business activity and prosperity caused in the great centers the accumulation of more money than the capitalist could lend in those centers to those they believed it safe to trust, could the enterprising men of the country borrow money on the security of their farms and their town property. When the active business men of those large communities made such sales of the commodities in which they dealt, and the purchasers of such commodities quickly paid for them, the banks were frequently unable to lend the money of their depositors; it remained idle in the vaults. At such times the managers of these banks turned their search for users of their money to centers other than their own. All the great commercial and financial centers were alike affected with a redundancy of money. Hence it was the weaker centers toward which those bank managers then looked for users of their money. To follow step by step the process by which their financial eyes rested upon Illustrateville is not necessary. We will, however, turn to the method by which they reached a like community. Some fifteen or twenty miles away from such a community— in a country town, perhaps—were long established and thoroughly responsible banks. To the managers of those banks word was conveyed, by methods known to the money-lenders, that they could go to the great cities and borrow such sums of money, limited only by their credit, at very low rates of interest; this money they could have the use of for an indefinite time, subject, however, to a call-notice that must be given sixty or ninety days previously to the time when payment might be demanded. Flattering inducements were made frequently to the country banker: it would be many months, perhaps years, before the loan would be called in. Why? The city-bank managers had faith in the financial integrity of the country banker, and so felt perfectly safe in making such loans. In many cases banks borrowed money for less than two per cent. It was in such financial and business conditions of the country that many country banks aided in the organization of home industries. They lent on bonds and on mortgages on real estate the amount required to equip the plants and to purchase raw material for beginning operations, charging the legal interest—from two to six per cent. profit —for such loans as they had made of the money they had borrowed. Imagination may be left free to conjecture the oiliness of the country bankers' tongues when they aided in the promotion of enterprises in which they saw an opportunity for their banks to make a profit of three or four per cent. on the capital of the enterprise; promoted, too, without incurring a probable financial risk.

When the money of the business men of the great centers—deposited and not used in the great banks of the city, and not needed by them—had found its way through the country banks into the hands of the owners of country property, manufacturing industries were begun, and the towns in which such industries were started became apparently prosperous. These industries gave not only employment to the labor and the skill available in the community in which the town was situated, but they also drew citizens from other communities. As rapidly as finished the manufactured goods were sold readily and profitably, and the demand for more goods than the capacity of the plants could produce

frequently led to the enlargement of the factories. More money then was borrowed.

Why not? Satisfactory profits had been
made; the town had been improved; all its
people had become active workers at profitable occupations; why should not the managers of the industry borrow more money,
enlarge their opportunity for profit and for the
development of the town? That was the way
business was done in the great cities; that
was the only way that men in manufacturing
avocations had ever lifted themselves from
lowly conditions to great wealth.

Generally, about the time that the additions
to the plant had all been finished, the man-
ager of it discovered he had greater difficulty
in effecting sales; it was quite possible, in fact,
for the old plant to have produced all of the
commodities that they could sell at a profit.
Collections became more difficult, and those
whom they owed were more anxious to make
collections. For a new tariff bill had been
projected by men of influence in the land; or
some hot-headed naval or commercial officer
in foreign lands had been subjected to some
indignity, to avenge which the " honor of the
nation " demanded that war should be declared. Or some great political organization
had determined that the best policy for the
Government to pursue in regard to its mone-

tary system was something radically different from the existing system; or one of a multitude of other causes had affected public confidence in business men's ability to fulfill their contracts.

That lack of confidence would be indicated first in the great centers. The most cowardly thing of all things cowardly is money; and the larger the amount of money, the bigger the coward. The great banks of the city would very early in the disturbance call in their loans to the country banks. And the country banks would have no option in the matter. Not only would they be compelled to refuse to the country factory further aid, in the shape of new loans and discounts, but the country bank would be compelled to demand the payment of most of the mortgages given by the individual stockholders of the factory on their private holding. Before anyone but the skillful financial operator of the great cities had learned that a depressed condition of business might be expected, the manufacturing enterprises of the town in illustration would be financially ruined. By the ease with which they borrowed money they had been " charmed " into an unnatural development of industries in their town; " charmed " into additional improvement by the apparently satisfactory profits on the earliest efforts; they had stretched their credits to the uttermost, and when the frost of business depression fell, they were powerless. The commodities they had manufactured in excess of orders—and under the conditions it was quite natural that the supply should be large—were forced upon the market at ruinous prices, to meet pressing demands for money. The works were closed, because goods could not be sold at even the cost of production; the vast plant became of no value unless the business could be continued; not ten per cent. of its cost could be realized under a forced sale. Although the factory became idle, the interest-account never ceased to grow, except when payments on it were made. The people who had been attracted to the town when the business of the factory was active could not pay rents, and houses became unoccupied and dilapidated rapidly. People who had become educated to active work and good wages became idlers and grumblers; the merchants of the town, one by one, were compelled to give up business or make terms with their creditors.

In communities where such disaster prevailed real estate would naturally depreciate. Measured, too, by the ability of its owners to borrow money on it, the depreciation would be to a point below that which existed at the

time the promoting of manufacturing industries there was first discussed.

This is not a fanciful illustration; it is real.
And it is within the bounds of truth to say that
upward of a thousand of such communities
exist to-day in the United States. And too
frequently the blighted hopes of the business
men who promoted those industries, united
with the great disappointment of the wage-
earners of the community, have resulted in a
perceptible lowering of the moral condition
of those communities.

CHAPTER X.

WE will now return to Illustrateville, during the prevalence of a monetary system predicated on justice; a system that gives opportunity to all and is unjust to none, whether the measure of value be of gold or of silver. This the Government regulates as it regulates the yardstick. Upon the latter the Government stamps its guarantee of the accuracy of the measure, and charges those who may need it the cost of the stamping. But, as the cost of coining gold is an infinitesimal part of the value of the metal used, there may perhaps be no objection to Governmental free coinage.

For the convenience of interstate travelers, and men of other businesses who might demand money that could be used throughout the country, the United States might issue paper bills about equal in volume to the issue of the silver notes now in circulation; bills that would be received by the Government for taxes and custom duty, but not necessarily to be legal tender for any other purpose. And it would be more desirable if the issue of such paper-substitute for money be limited to at

least one-half of the annual expenses of the
general Government.

Such bills of the Government—because of
their convenience for so many purposes
where gold coins would be inconvenient—
would, anywhere in the United States and
at all times, be equal in value to the standard
money. It is assumed that the standard will
be the present gold dollar. Of such limited
paper money not enough could be had
by taxpayers with which to pay all taxes
and customs, and the amount of such substitutes for money furnished by the Government should always be so limited that
not enough of it could be had at any time to
meet the requirement of the taxpayers. This
would require that taxpayers pay some part
of their taxes in gold dollars. It would
be a faulty monetary system should the Government require that a part of the taxes be
paid in gold. When offered by the taxpayer,
the Government should accept its tax notes in
full payment; but if the issue of these notes
were limited to one-half the annual budget,
there would be a constant flow of gold into the
Treasury, and, in all probability, a percentage
of taxes would be paid in that metal far greater
than by the use of tax notes. These not
being legal tenders, could be put into circulation only by the Government using them—

to purchase commodities and pay for services rendered to the Government. To the Government might safely be given the option of paying its debts with these tax notes, excepting those already contracted for, and for which gold payment was pledged. For governments should always redeem their pledges. There would be no trouble, however, to get the notes into circulation. They would readily be accepted in this country by all to whom they were offered; and it is quite possible that, at times, they might command a premium of a fraction f one per cent. For, so long as the Government lasts and receives them for taxes they would never be discounted. This truth is so axiomatic that any argument to prove it would be ridiculous. The tax note would never menace the credit of the nation. The Government would be under no obligation to redeem any of its circulating tax notes, except as they flowed into the Treasury through the channels of taxation. Its credit, therefore, would not be disturbed by any effort of the owners of gold coins and of bullion to disturb the value of that metal. These owners could appreciate or depreciate the metal used for standard coin without any disturbance to the Government's finances, although any disturbance of the value of the metal of the standard would affect the business operations of the country more or less seriously. But all would be affected alike—from the Atlantic to the Pacific, from the Gulf to the Great Lakes.

When the measure of value was the present gold dollar, Illustrateville organized to promote home industries. The Government's only paper issues were tax notes, redeemable by the Government only for taxes and customs dues, and not legal tenders for any other obligations of the people; when no obstructions in the way of private or of State banks were imposed by the United States; when the Government of nation or State did not guarantee the redemption of paper money, and to make a bank bill sound used no methods besides those used to secure the payment of any other kind of an I. O. U.

In fact, any other kind of Government paper money that would serve the purpose of currency that tax notes accomplish, would not interfere with the operations of banks like the one under illustration.

The necessity to provide useful and profitable occupations for the young men and women of Illustrateville (for upward of four hundred of them in the community were so anxious to do something for themselves that they were preparing to go away to larger business centers, or to the great cities) had been long discussed by lawyers, doctors, ministers, merchants, mechanics, and farmers of the community. Those discussions were keenly listened to by the young people who loved so well the place of their birth. But they felt impelled by necessity to leave it for opportunities to earn a sustenance; and so it was with the keenest delight that they hailed the crystallization of that long discussion—a real effort to establish a factory in Illustrateville.

Of the community of which Illustrateville was the center the more enterprising citizens, who possessed valuable real estate and improvements thereon, met in the town hall, or, perhaps, in the schoolhouse, to discuss plans.

Soon it was ascertained that there were not sufficient gold dollars or tax notes in the possession of the community to accomplish anything of a practical nature. It was suggested that some of the real-estate holders borrow money on their real estate, and lend it to the proposed company, on the security, perhaps, of the stock of the company. The objection to this plan was soon apparent. No property-owner would incur the risk of borrowing money to lend to a prospective company, unless he could, to a great extent, control the company. And none among those best able to raise money by mortgaging their real estate, cared to impose upon themselves the burden of a business of which they knew practically but little.

It was determined finally to organize a bank. It was not necessary to have any gold or tax notes. The possession of a few thousand dollars' worth would be an advantage, but not a real necessity. It was, however, necessary to have honest and capable managers of that bank; men well known to the community of Illustrateville for their keen business perspicuity, sterling integrity, and sobriety.

To avoid difficulties, annoyances, and disturbance of business it was determined that it would be better to organize the bank as a corporation rather than as a firm. These annoyances and difficulties would necessarily occur whenever death claimed one of the members of the firm, and that would be likely to occur frequently, as there would necessarily be a large number of members of the banking company, and they would almost all be men who had practically fought the battles of life and were retired veterans.

The charter of the Bank of Illustrateville was secured. A vigorous man of the town was made president. Years of careful attention to his business—that of a country merchant, perhaps—and a life of sobriety, in-

dustry, and integrity, had won for him success
and the confidence of the public generally.

He was selected by a board of directors, all
men well known in the community, and generally respected for their many good qualities.
A cashier was then appointed, a young man of
honesty and sobriety, whose father and grand-
father had been well acquainted with most of
the older men of the community, and were
known to be honest and worthy. All the employees of the bank were well known, at least
to the business people of Illustrateville; consequently, when the bank opened its doors, the
character of its officers had inspired the public with the belief that so long as the bank remained under the same management, nothing
would be done to impair its credit. Those
citizens who aided in the organization of that
bank did not care a rap about establishing a
credit for the bank elsewhere than in the community, for whose convenience, and for the
promoting of new industries of which, it had
been organized. Those of the management
who were anxious for profits could not have
been induced to resort to unnatural means to
establish a credit elsewhere, as there would
be no possibility of making profits from promoting such credits sufficient to compensate
for any expense of artificially doing so. For,
having no money to lend, nor seeking to bor-

row, there would be no way by which profits
for the bank could be realized from distant
centers. The great object of the bank was to
promote home industries, not to make profits
by lending money, although profits could reasonably be expected by the bank's management as the result of the promotion of those
industries.

The plans for promoting those industries
were very simple. Within the community of
Illustrateville raw material—for the purpose
of manufacturing the articles that were proposed should be manufactured at home—
could, it was known, be readily obtained. The
skill and labor were there, largely in idleness,
and all that was necessary to make the finished
article was to provide the ways and means by
which skill and labor could so manipulate the
raw material as to produce the finished product. It would not be necessary that all the
raw material should be accessible within the
limits of the community, because the bank's
credit was sufficient to bring it from other sections, and the finished product of the factory
could readily be exchanged for gold money.

The bank was organized by issuing stock
to those possessors of real estate in the community who wished to become stockholders.
The stockholders paid for their shares of stock
by giving to the bank mortgages—always the

first—on their real-estate holding. Stock would not be issued on real estate for more than one-third or less of its market value. Such mortgages did not bear interest, and could at any time be liquidated by the holder of such mortgages paying to the bank in gold or tax notes, or notes of the bank, the amount of the mortgage, or by surrendering the stock.

But the bank agreed that money so paid should be re-lent, as expeditiously as safety would permit, to some real-estate owner who would accept the stock of the bank in exchange for the mortgage. It would be very rare when there would be any such transfers of mortgages, for the selling value of such mortgaged places would be more likely to advance in price than be affected otherwise. The stock issued against the mortgaged property would naturally be transferred to any purchaser of such mortgaged property, and, being profit-making stock, it would generally add additional value to the mortgaged land. Various other valuable plans for organization of the Bank of Illustrateville might have been accepted by its originators, inasmuch as at the time the bank was organized there were no laws standing as impediments in the way of banks whose capital was gold or any other commodity established.

But, there was very little cash capital

available in the community, and as the commodity of gold served no better purposes in promoting financial credit than improved real estate, these holders of real estate, and not of gold, chose real estate to be the basis of their financial credit. When the bank was finally established, these holders held mortgages to the amount of one hundred thousand dollars against from three to four hundred thousand dollars' worth of real estate, all of which was improved and occupied.

Probably the stock was distributed among fifty holders. None held very large amounts. Those who aided in the bank's organization were men past middle age; they had grown up in the community and knew every stockholder in the bank; knew every foot of land against which these mortgages rested. Not one could neglect his holding or, by inattention or any other cause, permit it to depreciate without all the other stockholders being made acquainted with the facts. All were keenly alive to the importance; all were interested; each should maintain the value of the real estate against which the bank held mortgages. Under such system the bank possessed the power to call in the mortgages, and to demand payment in stock—the stock issued in exchange for the mortgages—therefore, a depreciation of the securities constituting the bank's capital was impossible. Should the bank be overtaken by disaster, its stock would, to the extent of its full face-value, be made available to pay its liabilities. But disaster was almost impossible, as will be shown later.

The bank was successfully organized. Had there been any necessity for the use of money, the credit and the character of the men who managed it, aided by the valuable mortgages they held, would have secured a loan of the necessary amount. But in the case of the industry proposed, when almost the entire cost was for labor and raw material, which the community possessed, money was not necessary, but for the convenience of all the people of the community of which Illustrateville was the center, the bank issued a substitute for money that was nothing more or less than a bank bill that none were compelled to take as payment for commodities sold or services rendered, but which all dwelling in the community, for whose convenience it was issued, would, nevertheless, readily accept. On its face it read, " The bank of Illustrateville will pay to bearer, on demand, the sum of one dollar." Everyone there felt confident that when a demand was made on the bank for that dollar it would be satisfied, and that, every dollar called for on the face of the note would be paid in gold dollars or tax notes. A demand for the dollar, under such circumstances, would seldom be made; only when people wanted to go away from Illustrateville would they demand gold, or request tax notes, in exchange for their bank bills.

Four or five active, intelligent, industrious, sober, and honest young men—no other kind would receive any attention from the bank officers—proposed to erect in Illustrateville a factory, in which to manufacture fruit baskets and plaque ware. This will prove as good an industry for illustration as anything else. Other men would organize for the manufacture of other commodities. The young men were known to the managers of the bank. It would be useless for any whose character could not have stood the most rigid investigation to have applied to the bank for financial aid. The success of the bank depended upon the character of the men financially aided by it, as well as upon any other kind of securities. Hence, sobriety, industry, intelligence, and integrity, when united in one individual, became capital worth more to that bank than any other kind of capital, because it possessed brains and energy. Such men could, with advantage to themselves, to the bank, and to the community, use those bank notes or certificates of credit that the bank must lend to realize profits.

For the erecting of the factory building but little money was needed. The bank notes would be received by the owners and the cutters of the timber and lumber used in the construction of the factory. All artisans and laborers engaged upon it accepted payment in the bank's notes; the merchants of the community readily accepted them in payment for those commodities that they sold. Money necessary for the purchase of the machinery could be furnished by the bank in notes given as security and secured by the indorsement of such men of property as might be interested in the success of the enterprise, and were acceptable to the managers of the bank.

As soon as the factory had been put into operation, the sale of its products would necessarily return to the town as much or more money than would be needed, so long as the bank's notes were freely accepted. The trees, from which the slats and veneering were procured, had been paid for with notes of the bank. The labor of cutting the trees from the stump had been paid for in those notes. The labor of manufacturing had been paid for by bank notes; also the labor of boxing and loading into cars, together with the skill that directed the work. All had been paid for with these notes. Only the nails and metal needed in the manufacturing had required any kind of money other than money's substitute in the character of those bank notes. The railroad company might or might not demand gold or tax notes in payment of freight; but of that invoice, amounting to one thousand dollars in value, the goods of which had been shipped to a great center and sold by the managers of that factory, all the expenses incurred in producing them and in placing them on the market in which they were to be consumed were—excepting perhaps fifty or seventy-five dollars at the utmost—liquidated by the use of those notes that had been issued by the Bank of Illustrateville, and readily received by the people of that community as of equal value with the gold money of the Government. They were accepted wherever received, because they would purchase as much commodities or labor as money of gold would procure.

Here we have an illustration of a community that possesses all materials—the products of nature and idle men and women—as possibilities for the production of wealth. As long as the labor remained idle there could be no production of wealth, and, of course, little or no progress. The community could not command gold or money to set energy in motion to produce wealth. Had money been advanced by capitalists from other centers, it is true wealth would have been produced;

but at what cost to that community? The
labor employed by those capitalists would
have been wage-earning, and to the extent
that wage-earning benefits communities
Illustrateville would have been improved.
Labor's share of gross earnings is rarely more
than twenty-five per cent. of the wealth it
creates in factories. All profits from such factories, which outside capital would have
operated in Illustrateville, would have gone
away from the town most probably, and no
improvement to the community would result
from the profits realized by such manufacturing. The products of nature—a part,
and frequently an important part, of the wealth
of a community—would also have been taken
from it; and to that extent, at least, the community would have been impoverished.

Being in possession of the right to organize a bank, and by organizing one for the loan
of its credit, in shape of currency-demand
notes, the people were enabled to convert
products of nature, practically useless to them
in the shape that nature finished them, into
valuable commodities, by employing idle
labor that, when idle, was a disadvantage to
the community. By combining nature's
products, by the employment of an impover-
ishing population,—idle people,—they practically increased the wealth of the community

to the full extent of the value of the commodities created, less the expenses of marketing them. This would be true absolutely in the case in illustration if the laborers, when employed, consumed no more commodities than when idle, and when no one hitherto employed was engaged in producing those commodities, but had been living upon the product of the labor of others of that community.

Illustrateville manfactured not only baskets and plaque ware; various other industries were promoted by the bank; fully enough to keep at home all who wished to remain in the place of their birth and be profitably employed. It had a foundry there that utilized the old iron mechanism that had been discarded and was practically useless. The new pig iron necessary for the new business would probably have to be bought with money other than the bills of the bank. All other cost of the finished product of the factory could unquestionably have been bought by the bank's notes. The products of its brickyards were created solely by the bank's credit currency. In extent and in embellishments Illustrateville grew rapidly. The factories created practically from nothing—unused natural products and hitherto idle labor—perhaps as much as four dollars' worth of commodities per day for each person employed, or nearly, or quite, two thousand dollars daily of really substantial wealth, one-fourth of which, under ordinary circumstances, would be accumulated in the shape of new or improved possessions of the people of the community that created the wealth. The interest paid to the managers of the bank, the profits realized by the managers of the factories, together with the wages and salaries paid, all would be retained in Illustrateville, a town of three thousand people, the center of a community of perhaps not over ten thousand. Thus, from their manufacturing industries alone, they would realize a profit of six or seven hundred thousand dollars per year above what they could possibly have accumulated had not such a bank as described promoted and developed those factories.

Nor would that measure the extent of the benefit to the community from such a source; because the seven thousand people living around about Illustrateville would also have received many benefits—a result of the prosperity of the town. No argument is necessary to prove this; its truth must be admitted by the thoughtful.

The town and community would prosper so long as markets could be found for their wares; they would be in a condition to manu-

facture at a minimum cost so long as the raw
material could be produced in the community
as cheaply as elsewhere, and so long as there
was not an excessive demand for labor there.
Labor could not command more wages than
the profits from the sales of the wares would
permit the manufacturers to pay. There is a
period that seems inevitably to occur in every
business when the product of factories cannot be sold at a profit, because in the markets
are offered, at a price that will not return
profits to the manufacturers, more of the
goods than consumers can use.

When that period arrived, the manufacturers of Illustrateville would either shut
down their works or reduce the output, by
shortening hours of work, or by employing
fewer workers, until scarcity of their wares in
the market would raise the selling price to a
point where profits would be returned to
them.

This they could readily do. The bank held
their obligations; the management of the bank
would never have permitted them to extend
their business beyond a legitimate risk. The
money they had borrowed was the credit of
the bank. The bank had borrowed no money
to promote those industries; no capitalists, no
other bank, could demand of the Bank of Illustrateville the amount of money that that bank

had lent to those manufacturers of the town
to promote the industries now embarrassed
for the lack of customers.   It was a necessity
of the bank to maintain the various industries
that its credit had promoted.   It might possess the power to close some of them out, perhaps all of them, but it could not be to its
advantage to do so; it would, probably, be to
its disadvantage. The bank could make profits
only by lending its credit, excepting from that
little that could be made by lending its excess deposits.   Unless, indeed, factories were
to be operated in the future, the bank could
not hope to find a future market for its credit.

Should the bank close any one of the industries it had promoted, it would have to do so
because the management of that industry had
failed, in some way, to show good business
qualities, or, in the minds of such men as the
banks must lend its credit to, it would impair
faith in the fairness and in the good business
qualifications of the bank's management.
Without this faith in the bank no man of such
capabilities as the bank must necessarily use
would undertake to build an industry promoted by it.

The bank, being under no pressure from
without, could afford to permit all of these industries to remain idle. Its stock cost nothing;
stockholders would simply have less profits;

their stock would be unimpaired; it was really only a part of their farms and houses. They could be put to only a slight cost even if the bank remained in idleness, together with the factories; for the expense of maintaining the bank would be light. The money that the bank had borrowed, if any, upon which interest was being paid, could readily be returned or lent elsewhere, to produce interest with which to pay interest. The currency of the community would be bank bills of Illustrateville, so long as the people of the community had faith in the integrity of the bank, and those bills would reach the bank only to pay an indebtedness to the bank or as a deposit. If each man in the community had in his possession ten dollars of these bills, there would be not over twenty or twenty-five thousand dollars of them out. The merchants of the community might have as much more again on deposit in the bank. All of these bills—those in circulation and those in the bank—might be interest-earning to the bank, but the bank's liabilities for i⁺ circulating notes would not be one-tenth of its real assets. Every obligation of the bank would be represented by its circulating notes and its deposits. It would rarely lend anything but its credit—as represented by these notes—to those to whom it extended a credit. It never borrowed. For all the notes it issued, or lent, it received pledges of security that they, or legal-tender money, would be returned to the bank in liquidation of the lo¬n.

The bank managers would not consent to have manufactured products sold at ruinous prices to provide the manufacturer with means to pay his obligations to the bank. Nor would they consent to excessive or speculative productions. To do so would not be good business. If a manufacturer were in possession of sufficient wealth to do this without the bank's aid, then the bank would have no further use of him; and his failure, therefore, could not affect the bank. If he persisted in manufacturing with his own means, or means borrowed from outside capitalists, the bank would not lose anything from a disaster that might overtake him, and Illustrateville would be benefited to the extent to which outside capital may have been absorbed by the town in such unprofitable productions, less such interest that may have been paid for the use of that outside capital.

It will be seen, then, that it is possible to have a bank of issue that will provide a medium of exchange; that will enable hitherto idle labor to manipulate nature's products into useful commodities, without that bank having any capital other than real estate. This, of course, any community of civilization can furnish. It has been shown that, in the community in which the bank is situated, and for the convenience of which it was established, such a bank can provide a currency equal in value to the best currency of the world, but of so little value elsewhere that it will not be received as money by anyone who does not intend to use it in the vicinity of the bank that issued it. And no one excepting the management of the bank, and then only at the office of the bank, is compelled to accept it.

The history of Illustrateville demonstrates that such a currency can practically produce wealth from that which is more worthless for the time being than nothing—useless natural products and idle labor; that it can stimulate industries to a point the commercial world is pleased to term overproduction, and can then in safety stop the business of production until a scarcity of products in communities creates wants that will return profits, and during the period of waiting nothing of past labor's productions is sacrificed. It has been demonstrated also that under that system, the condition of labor has been so advantageous that only the most wretched recklessness, due to accumulated rewards, could have prevented the employee from awaiting the coming of the revived business. It has been shown, too, that during the period of manufacturing activity, under the system described, the accumulation; of wealth have been reserved for the people of the communities that created it, and distributed it, as fairly as under any system of economy yet devised.

It has also been shown that, under the system of money now prevalent in the world, and particularly in the United States, the profit realized for most of the industries developed in the country districts,—more especially those remote from great centers,—have been taken from the communities that yielded them; that frequently more than profits have been absorbed by other communities; that the accumulation of those instrumental in organizing, in a limited way, small industries, have gone to those who aided them with capital to extend their plant, and that when the period of "overproduction" and stringent money market came the industries have frequently been crushed out, the community impoverished, and the people demoralized. But the great centers have grown in extent of territory, of magnificence, rich men, poverty, crime, and degradation.

When the Government is confined to its legitimate functions, completely separated from the banking business, a paper currency, as has been shown, can be issued that will afford to all sections of our country a safe and elastic bank currency. But not one uniform and under Government supervision, and where there is also no need of the Government to exert itself to measure the volume by the needs of business.

If the civilized governments will confine their monetary laws to defining the quantity of the measuring metal the unit of value must contain, and permit the methods of expediting exchange of commodities to be adjusted by tradesmen's business necessities and capabilities, a paper substitute for money will be provided that will be as effective in promoting exchanges as any other possible means. Of this there can be no reasonable doubt.

The needs of business will do its own measuring accurately, while the Government's would never be correct unless by an occasional accident. It would be a paper currency, not made legal tender for public and private debts, but as good, where issued, as the best money of the world. Under a perfectly free banking system the volume of currency in circulation would be regulated entirely by the demands of communities for it. Those communities that might at one season of the year demand the use of $150,000 of circulating bills, and at another time not

$50,000, would be accommodated with currency by the free banks according to the community's wants. When the community needed $150,000 of the currency bills, the bank would lend its credit to that amount, and from the loan of its credit make the same profits that it could have made from the loan of $150,000 of gold coin. But as gold would have been capable of earning interest without the bank's credit sustaining it, the bank would be compelled to lose whatever interest its gold was capable of earning when it retained the gold in its vault, or whenever it was unlent.

Not so with its credit bills. If the interest on loans were six per cent., as long as the bank could lend $150,000 of currency notes, it made from the loans of its credit $750 per month, less the bank's expense;—not from the loan of accumulated wealth. When the business of the community demanded only a few thousand dollars' worth of currency notes, the bank's profits would be little or nothing. But why should the bank derive a profit from its business with a community so embarrassed for the want of consumers of its wares as to be compelled to resort to idleness to avoid losing the wealth it had already accumulated; a community forced to idleness that economies essential to its future prosperity might be accomplished? Why should the commodity of money, or the commodity of land—the bank's capital—possess a privileg? not common to all other commodities?

It may occur to some minds that the Bank of Illustrateville might, at some period in its history, when it had issued a very large amount of currency notes, be embarrassed by an impairment of its credit, and it might even have the greater part of its notes offered at its counter for redemption in gold; but such a condition would be only a remote possibility to the bank. Should outside capitalists, seeking to injure it, be willing to pay dearly for the pleasure of doing so, it might cause the bank to close its business for a time; but so long as the bank's managers possessed the confidence of the trading public of their town, the inconvenience to the business of the bank and the community would be but for a short time.

The bank could readily realize sufficient cash on its valuable holdings of real estate and other collaterals, which it had taken from every man to whom it had issued a note; and when it had done so, its notes could all be paid. It then would not owe a dollar. The money it had borrowed to redeem its notes would have been repaid from the collections of the debts owed to the bank, which would be in exactly the same condition to do business as it had been on the day it first opened its doors. If outside capitalists had been able to command one hundred thousand dollars of the notes, they could have accumulated those notes only by slowly purchasing and by holding them. The Bank of Illustrateville would probably be making interest on these notes all the while that those seeking to injure the bank were holding them. For those notes might be interest-making so long as they remained outside of the bank that issued them. They could be had only by purchase at their full face-value. The gold with which they would have to be purchased would go to those in Illustrateville who used the bank's circulating notes, and in the usual course of business would naturally go into the bank's vaults through the channel of bank deposits. This would to a great extent furnish the bank with gold to meet any demands made upon it for the redemption of its notes. The managers of the bank would know whenever such an effort to secure an extraordinary amount of its notes was being made, because the needs of the business of the town for currency notes would be apparent to them, and whenever an excessive number of their notes were in circulation they would well know that an unusual and senseless movement was taking place; they would therefore naturally reserve a corresponding amount of the gold that those persons who were hoarding their notes foolishly provided the bank with.

It is not to be supposed that the officers, whose qualifications and integrity had inspired confidence among the people of a community to accept their currency notes at a value equal to the best money in the country, would lend those notes on the security of irresponsible people, just for the sake of getting those notes into circulation. The bank could not make anything by it. It is quite possible that if they did lend their notes recklessly, the bank would not be able to collect a dollar from those irresponsible persons to whom they made the loans. It would rather be compelled to pay out a gold dollar for each dollar's worth of those notes that it had lent to irresponsible persons. The managers of the bank, therefore, would be just as particular regarding the responsibility of those to whom they lent their credit notes as they would if they had had nothing but gold money to lend.

Irresponsible men could not organize such banks. As it has already been said: having no credit, they could not sell credit. No one would take their notes. They could not circulate currency. The conditions would not be those that existed in the United States in 1860, when there was no paper money that was good money in every community of the entire country, and when the conveniences for the use of gold and silver were not nearly so great as now, and when there was almost no clearing-house system for the banks of the country. But with a national paper money as good as gold, although not a legal-tender money, with a telegraphic and telephonic system, that practically brings in twenty-four hours at the most any bank of the country into communication with that bank that is furthest away from it, there can be no such confusion as that which was so objectionable in the old State banks. If the people of the United States will not accept a bank bill of Canada, which is redeemable in the United States gold dollar, it is unreasonable to assume that the people of New York would accept a bank bill of a private bank of Philadelphia, or even of Newark, N. J., in payment of a debt due them, when they have a right to demand, and can readily get, money that would be perfectly acceptable to them. To a creditor no bills would be acceptable that he did not feel confident could be exchanged for an equal amount of the best money in use. No creditor would take money of any kind that was not so good as the standard money.

Banks, as a matter of self-interest—under a system where all bank-note currency is furnished by free banks—would, as speedily as possible, return to the banks that issued them the notes that came to them in the usual course of business. The notes of other banks could not conveniently nor profitably be used by the bank that received them, hence they, with the speediest dispatch possible, would be returned to the bank that issued them for redemption. They would be treated just as checks drawn on other banks are now treated, and a demand for payment in gold would at once be made on the issuing bank. The reason is very clear. Banks, under a free-banking system, can make more profit from lending their credit in the shape of their currency notes than from any other loans they can make. To pay out to depositors the notes of other banks only reduces their own opportunity to lend their own notes, for their notes are lent and are earning interest whenever in the hands of others as circulating notes. If other notes displace theirs, they fail to make profits, to the extent that such circulation of other notes or money prevents their own notes from earning interest.

A few words shall be said here that may lead some who are doubtless prejudiced against free banking—because of their recollection of the bank notes that served the United States with currency from 1832 to

1863—to a more careful analysis of the conditions of the people of the agrarian districts of this country during those years.

New England had during that time become a great cotton-manufacturing community, rivaling England in the world's market for cotton fabrics. Pennsylvania had so advanced her industries in iron that the finished articles of her industries in that metal were to be found in use in all quarters of the globe, and American railroad engines were extensively used in Europe, specially in Russia.

American clocks were, during that time, sold in all parts of the world, even in Switzerland to a very great extent. American ships carried the flag of the American commerce wherever there was a navigable sea or a channel for trade. American prosperity invited the best blood of Europe to our shores, which aided to build up a mighty empire west of the thirteen original States. In that period a cable was laid across the Atlantic Ocean by American enterprise, uniting us in closer ties to the civilizations of Europe. Thousands of miles of railroads were built and operated, bringing under cultivation millions of acres of hitherto unproductive lands. The free-school system could be found in every community, and together with the church extension and the development of the printing press, the

young of the land were thereby taught principles of sobriety, integrity, and industry.
And when the calamity of the Civil War fell
upon the land it disclosed that never before in
the history of the world had a people been
more perfectly instructed in those cardinal
virtues. They fought battles for principle, and
not because of hate. And when the war ended,
the contending forces clasped hands across
the bloody chasm, and, as friendly rivals, began a new contest for the restoration of a
common country to prosperity and greatness;
a contest in which sword and cannon gave
place to a geater force,—sobriety, integrity,
and industry in concert.

Now it would not be fair to assert that all
the greatness and prosperity that our country
enjoyed during the period when banking was
comparatively free in the United States, was
the result of that banking system. It is nevertheless fair to contend that the free-banking
system that prevailed, when only States au-
thorized those banks that furnished all the
paper currency in use, did not retard the progress of the country; that the system did not
develop poverty and crime; did not lower the
standard of morals and education, and did not
oppress any community of the country.

It is true that some unwise men and women
received in payment, during the period of

wild-cat money, some bills that were not worth anything; but it by no means follows that because of this the benefit derived from free banking was not far more than compensation for its defects. The person who pays to another a worthless bill, however innocent of an intention to do so, is not relieved from the debt, and he must give good money for the worthless money before the debt can be liquidated. To make laws to prevent men from being swindled has never been successfully accomplished. To make laws to punish swindlers is an easy task.

There seems always to have been a large class of people who have shown great ingenuity in discovering new ways to be swindled. The swindlers of the world are not half so prolific in inventing new schemes of swindling as those who seem desirous of being swindled are in arriving at the means by which they can enjoy that sensation. To inconvenience one hundred men in order to prevent one from being imposed upon, is not good ethics. There are those who will never learn from the wisdom of others, but will investigate for themselves. The bunco steerer is perhaps, all things considered, a useful teacher of many who were once his victims. It is even possible that he has taught so many useful lessons that he has benefited more than injured society. His victims needed more thorough instruction than public schools and books and newspapers could give them; and they needed that instruction badly.

A people who acknowledge themselves to be so stupid that they fear to trust themselves to determine the value of a currency note, but demand that a good, attentive paternal Government shall do it for them, need possibly the bunco steerer as a teacher before they can be put into possession of enough intelligence to enable them to produce their own sustenance. And a people who demand that laws be passed to make them good, will probably steadily degenerate. Persons who assert that they themselves are perfectly good, but demand laws to be enacted to compel others to do right, need watching to keep them out of lunatic asylums or out of prisons.

The natural man is too independent and self-reliant to listen willingly to the command "thou shalt not," while the admonition "thou shouldst not" appeals to his reason. He can be persuaded more readily than driven. The man that must be driven to do a generous deed can never do it without feeling a degree of resentment, which is most likely to result in his doing a most ungenerous deed to compensate him for what he believed he had lost.

Police laws should be made with the sole view of punishing criminals. It is almost a waste of time, thought, and material to formulate them to prevent men from committing crime. Education must do that. It is also a waste of time, thought, and energy to formulate laws to prevent foolish people from buying worthless commodities. Education alone can do that. As certainly as the threat of eternal punishment does not prevent those who believe in such punishment from breaking all of the Decalogue, nor that of death prevent murder, so certain is it that no threatened punishment will prevent foolish bargain hunters from purchasing useless and worthless commodities.

Paternalism in government has always retarded progress, and so long as it exists it will continue to do_so; to debase man's mental forces, enlarge immorality, and increase poverty and crime. Wherever those conditions exist in Christian lands, where good strong locks or guards are required to keep the public from stealing the church Bible, there will probably be found a good strong paternal government.

There are a thousand and one good reasons why the Government should keep its hands off the banking business, and permit the people to manage their own affairs. There is not one good reason why it should conduct a banking business or seek to control those who do.

There is, very generally, among business men and bankers, an objection to using real estate as security for currency circulation. But why should there be? There is doubly as much paper money in use in the world as there is gold with which to redeem it, and the gold is in such shape and under such control that it is quite probable that, if the entire world could, at the same time, be affected by such a scare as that given to the business men of the United States in October of last year, two-thirds of the gold would get into hands that would not permit it to be used in redeeming currency notes. The men who control the vast gold holdings of our country, of England, of France, of Germany, of Austria, and of Russia would stop paying gold when it should become apparent to them that a demand for the redemption in gold of the paper money in circulation would exhaust all their stores of gold, and still leave much paper money, representing millions of dollars of value, unpaid. And if it were necessary to conserve the interest of the large holders of gold early in the movement, means would be found to stop the redemption of the notes. It is not at all improbable that the very gold pledged to redeem the paper money might frequently be used to buy the discredited money; that profits also might be realized, just as the gold reserved by State banks in 1863 was used by those banks to buy legal-tender Government money at a discount, with which to redeem their own notes.

At the close of the last century, the banks of England were permitted to suspend specie payment for nearly twenty years, the gold of the banks being used for purposes other than to redeem notes with. Governments have always shown a remarkable promptness in aiding the owners of gold and silver to avoid fulfillments of contracts that are likely to deprive them of their specie, and the reason for so doing is readily apparent. Most of the governments of the world that afford us any knowledge of their monetary system have been monarchies, or governments of a privileged class, and such governments owe much of their existence to those who possess the money of the country, and it is but natural that the rulers should attend closely to the personal interests of those upon whom they depend so much to continue as rulers.

Real estate, pledged for the payment of a specific debt, cannot so readily escape the burden placed upon it as long as those obligations, in the shape of currency notes, rested against a bank the capital of which was real estate. If mortgaged for that specific purpose, the payment of those notes would be assured if the value of the real estate mortgaged was sufficient to realize the value of the circulating notes. The facts in regard to the volume of notes issued, and to the value of the real estate pledged, would be best known to those people living in close contact with the bank. Because of their faith in the ability of the bank to meet its notes on demand, they would readily be accepted as money when issued. And because such a faith can be sustained only by a knowledge of the facts, and, as those people living remote from the bank would not possess those facts, such notes would not be accepted by them as money.

Thieves may rob a bank of its gold reserve, and wreck it. Banks have been robbed of millions of their money and securities. The bank whose capital is mortgages on real estate cannot be robbed of its capital, and thieves have no use for unissued bills of a bank; they can scarcely use them as money without being detected in the crime of robbery.

It may be urged that such banks as that of Illustrateville are better suited to promote the industries of small communities than of great cities. That is true; and that is their real merit; but they do no injustice to the great cities. Strong financial communities, like great cities, can readily take care of themselves. They need no outside help, but they should never be permitted to put to an unjust cost outside communities. Injustice to themselves they can stand, and even be strong, but they nevertheless should not be submitted to such injustice.

They can have their own strong confederation of banks, the capital of which may be gold, Government and other such securities, or real estate; and they may have paper currency, common to all, or to individual banks. There would be no difficulty whatever in operating such banks in large cities. But it is for the people of those cities to say how they shall do business that does injustice to none. And to interfere with them is not the business of the Government.

THE END.